P9-AOR-915

FLORIDA STATE
UNIVERSITY LIBRARIES

JAN 12 1995

TALLAHASSEE, FLORIDA

Women and Work
in Developing Countries

Recent Titles in
Bibliographies and Indexes in Women's Studies

Women Writers of Germany, Austria, and Switzerland: An Annotated
Bio-Bibliographical Guide
Elke Frederiksen, editor

Immigrant Women in the United States: A Selectively Annotated
Multidisciplinary Bibliography
Donna Gabaccia, compiler

Women and the Literature of the Seventeenth Century: An Annotated
Bibliography Based on Wing's *Short Title Catalogue*
Hilda Smith and Susan Cardinale, compilers

Women and Mass Communications: An International Annotated Bibliography
John A. Lent

Sources on the History of Women's Magazines, 1792-1960: An Annotated
Bibliography
Mary Ellen Zuckerman, compiler

Feminist Research Methods: An Annotated Bibliography
Connie Miller with Corinna Treitel

War and Peace through Women's Eyes: A Selective Bibliography of
Twentieth-Century American Women's Fiction
Susanne Carter

American Women Playwrights, 1900-1930: A Checklist
Frances Diodato Bzowski, compiler

Women in Japanese Society: An Annotated Bibliography of Selected
English Language Materials
Kristina Ruth Huber, with Kathryn Sparling

United States Government Documents on Women, 1800-1990: A Comprehensive
Bibliography, Volume I: Social Issues
Mary Ellen Huls

United States Government Documents on Women, 1800-1990: A Comprehensive
Bibliography, Volume II: Labor
Mary Ellen Huls

Mothers and Daughters in American Short Fiction: An Annotated Bibliography
of Twentieth-Century Women's Literature
Susanne Carter, compiler

Women and Work in Developing Countries

An Annotated Bibliography

Compiled by
Parvin Ghorayshi

Bibliographies and Indexes in Women's Studies, Number 20
Dan A. Chekki, Series Adviser

Greenwood Press
Westport, Connecticut · London

Library of Congress Cataloging-in-Publication Data

Women and work in developing countries : an annotated bibliography /
  compiled by Parvin Ghorayshi.
      p. cm. – (Bibliographies and indexes in women's studies,
  ISSN 0742-6941 ; no. 20)
    Includes bibliographical references and index.
    ISBN 0-313-28834-8 (alk. paper)
      1. Women – Employment – Developing countries – Bibliography.
    2. Women – Developing countries – Economic conditions – Bibliography.
    I. Ghorayshi, Parvin. II. Series.
    Z7963.E7W655 1994
    [HD6223]
    016.3314'09172'4 – dc20   93-38803

British Library Cataloguing in Publication Data is available.

Copyright © 1994 by Parvin Ghorayshi

All rights reserved. No portion of this book may be
reproduced, by any process or technique, without the
express written consent of the publisher.

Library of Congress Catalog Card Number: 93-38803
ISBN: 0-313-28834-8
ISSN: 0742-6941

First published in 1994

Greenwood Press, 88 Post Road West, Westport, CT 06881
An imprint of Greenwood Publishing Group, Inc.

Printed in the United States of America

The paper used in this book complies with the
Permanent Paper Standard issued by the National
Information Standards Organization (Z39.48-1984).

10 9 8 7 6 5 4 3 2 1

To My Mother

and

To the Memory of My Grandmother

Contents

Preface

Work, the topic of this book, is one of the most sensitive and important issues of social life. Considerable changes have occurred over the past decade, both in the world of work and the academic analysis of the nature and condition of work in today's society. This field of study has increasingly become more complex and is covered by various disciplines and diverse theoretical frameworks, gradually building up an impressive body of knowledge. The growth in the study of work has provided fresh answers to the old questions, and raised novel issues as legitimate areas of investigation. Earlier studies on the world of work were updated in ways that took into account a number of complex social and economic developments, as well as the multidisciplinary nature of work. The result has been growing specialization and the development of sub-areas in the field of work.

One of the most important additions, as well as challenges, to the study of work has come from the growing interest in research on women and work. Feminist scholars have shown that women have a long history of engaging in productive work. Not only have women produced goods and services for their families' own consumption, they also have a long tradition of working for pay outside the home. However, the terms in which women participate in the labour force remain a considerable problem and are the central issue of debate among social scientists.

Scholars of women's studies have discussed the distinct nature of women's work and their differing pattern of participation in the labour force. They have widely documented that women's employment is segregated and concentrated in a limited number of low-paid occupations, and that women's work remains invisible. Women's invisibility and their unequal treatment are not limited to the studies of the labour market, but exist in all areas of social science. By focusing on women's issues, scholars have criticized research and theories on work for ignoring the experience of women as women and for downplaying women's experience as workers. Academic disciplines have been questioned, sometimes in their most basic self-conceptions and categories. The result has been a massive amount of literature and an increasing specialization within the field of women's studies itself. This growing specialization in women's studies, as in other academic disciplines, has produced a variety of sub-areas, such as women in literature, women in philosophy, feminist theory, and women in developing countries, to mention only a few.

Women's work in developing countries, the focus of this book, is one of the growing sub-areas of women's studies. Over the last three decades, scholars of women's studies have shown a particular interest in the study of women in developing countries. This interest reached its peak with the inauguration of the United Nations Decade for Women in 1975. Various UN agencies, the World Bank, many Western agencies for international development, private voluntary agencies, national states, women academics, and even multinational corporations identified with the field. As a result, during the past two decades, an impressive volume of research focused attention on the condition, lives and experiences of women in Africa, Asia, Latin America, the Caribbean and the Middle East. However, this expanding literature, for the most part, has dealt with women's lives and their status in society at the general level. Studies of women's working lives remain few and far between.

In this book, we have the arduous task of discussing

women's working lives in the developing countries. It is difficult to talk about women's work in developing countries as a whole without ignoring the vast economic, cultural, political and social differences between them. Such variations mean that although it is possible to make general statements about the relationship between work and gender, the use of a homogeneous definition of 'women's work' precludes an adequate explanation of either the structure of the labour market or the determinants of women's own self-perceptions and consciousness. The divisions of entries which focus on Africa, Asian, Latin America, the Caribbean and Middle East intend to take explicit account of the differences under which women work. This book makes the important point that the lives of women in Iran, for instance, are different from those in Ghana, Guatemala or India; and within countries, similar gaps in income, class, ethnicity and culture exist.

We acknowledge the differences in women's experiences of work, but stress the value of a comparative analysis of the conditions under which women work. Such a comparative perspective is necessary both for explaining inequality and for shedding light on the ways in which women's subordinate position is reinforced or can be challenged. Many previous studies have been related to women's position either in the developed or developing countries, implying a disjunction between the experiences of women in these distinct contexts. In this book, various sections of the chapters on Africa, Asia, Latin America, the Caribbean, and the Middle East allow us to compare women's position within and between geographic regions and to see both the similarities and differences among women's experiences. At the same time, variations in the specific position of women which relate to differences in economic, social, political and cultural contexts can be identified.

This book shows that unicausal explanations of women's working position are simplistic. Since women's unequal position results from, and is perpetuated by, a complex combination of factors, it is the analysis of the interrelationships between different factors which is appropriate. This means, most fundamentally, that women's interests and priorities are cut across by race, class,

ethnicity, and so on.   Rather than pretending unity, we must
recognize and confront the barriers to unity and try to overcome
the divisions that exist among women. We must consider, among
other things, the ways that structures of racism, sexism, class, and
other forms of oppression and their ideological formations are
historically implicated within a particular context. In doing so, we
will confront, rather than fear or ignore, the complexity of
women's experiences of oppression and the consequent differences
in women's priorities and concerns, and will thus maintain an
historically-based and contextual approach in analyzing women's
position. The entries demonstrate that as one moves from society
to society, women's position varies in form and content. One
cannot overemphasize this variability, for it points to the need for
considerable caution regarding the formulation and use of the many
generalizations that have been forwarded about the structure and
functioning of sexual ideologies.   These important differences
compel us to ask how differing social and material contexts interact
to produce a specific patriarchal system. On the other hand, the
entries exhibit compelling similarities regarding the assumptions
and attitudes toward women in various societies.

The central concern of this study is to develop an
understanding of the nature of women's work in all its variations
and permutations, and to evaluate its importance to the larger
society. In this original study we have gathered scattered literature
on women and work in developing countries and then have
logically divided it into sections, based on major themes emerging
from the research in this area since 1980, thus enabling users to
quickly access information related to their particular interests. The
entries presented in this book are about women's work, about the
structural factors which foster and/or limit their alternatives, and
about the effects of work on women's consciousness and lives.
Our approach will be interdisciplinary and informed of the fact that
women have always worked and contributed to the economy and
their households, in various ways. In order to fulfill this task, we
include those original studies that address the present themes,
debates, problems and issues regarding women's work in
developing countries. The entries have been chosen because they
make an important contribution to our understanding of women's

working lives. Special attention is paid to lines of studies that reveal the complexity and multi-dimensional nature of women's work.

Women and Work in Developing Countries crosses into a number of related disciplines. The unique feature of this volume is that it brings together some of the most significant achievements from different traditions since the 1980s. The entries with cross-references present students and researchers who are interested in the study of women's work in developing countries with examples of how different disciplinary approaches and research methods can be used to shed light on the complex nature of women's work. We draw from a variety of perspectives for studying the historical, economic, political, social and ideological nature of women's work. The entries go beyond a particular geographic area, bring diverse area studies, otherwise isolated projects, together, and show the similarities and differences in women's working lives in different parts of Africa, Asia, Latin America, the Caribbean and the Middle East. Although the focus is on the experience of women's work in developing countries, the entries make it clear that, in today's world, it is impossible to grasp the complexity of women's work in any single country in isolation from other societies.

We sought books, articles, reports, dissertations, videos and films that, together, would reflect a variety of perspectives and would shed light on multiple dimensions of women's work in contemporary developing countries. By relying on primary sources and drawing upon diverse disciplines, this annotated critical bibliography could serve as a research and reference tool for students, researchers, academics, policy makers, librarians, labour activists, women's groups, unions and the public at all levels. It will also help them to become more familiar with the current debate and to find their way into the literature on women's work in developing countries. The Appendix which contains the addresses of women's organizations and research centers is a valuable source for those who would like further information on women in a specific country or region.

We begin our examination by looking at general issues which are essential for understanding some of the major problems that face contemporary developing countries, and are, as a whole, relevant for doing research on women's work. The themes of the opening chapter, "General Works," are closely tied to the debates presented in each of the following chapters. The entries are concerned with the general discussion related to developing countries and are not specific to any particular country.

The section, "The Developing World and the Global Economy," brings out the impact of wider economic, political and social influences on workers, employers, unions and the state. The central theme emerging from the literature is the recognition of the fact that developing countries are incorporated into the global economy and that this integration affects women's working lives. A fundamental transformation has been taking place in the economic structure on a world scale. We have been witnessing a major shift towards the internationalization of capital and labour, facilitated by modern communications technology. Such a shift has implied a transition away from the classic international division of labour towards a restructured world economy, wherein developing countries are increasingly providing sites for industries that manufacture commodities for sale in the world economy. What is important to underline is that the integration of the world economy has eroded the significance of national boundaries and weakened the ability of individual countries to influence. This movement towards globalization of production and the creation of a global market has meant that the developing countries have acquired a new position within the international division of labour. As will be discussed in the following chapters, working women in developing countries are facing new challenges within the international division of labour. This challenge is particularly explicit when we look at women's work in Latin America.

The next theme of the first chapter, "Theoretical Considerations," is the debate on theory and method, the most pressing issues for the research on women's work. This section can serve as a guideline for doing research on women and work in both developed and developing countries. This discussion, as the entries make clear, has benefited from the contributions of scholars in both developed and developing countries. Research, both in the 'North' and in the 'South,' shows that such taken-for-granted concepts as 'work,' 'economically-active person,' and 'labour force participation' have not been defined in ways that capture the nature of women's roles in both productive and reproductive activities. National censuses in many countries seriously underestimate the economic role of women. Women remain 'invisible' in the official statistics and analysis that have formed the basis for a multitude of policies and programs. Definitions of work, usually in terms of salaried activities undertaken during a given calendar week called the 'reference week,' fail to capture many productive activities of women that are discontinuous, that is, part-time, seasonal, or performed concurrently with other tasks within the home. Moreover, definitions of 'participation' that are limited to the context of formally-organized, paid activities fail to consider women's participation in the informal sector of the economy. Such definitions have only tended to produce a picture of women as passive subjects and housewives.

"Voices from the Developing Countries" demonstrates that research on women in the 'South' is both strongly influenced by, and increasingly critical of, the feminist studies in the 'North.' Feminist literature has become the subject of severe criticism and lively debate. Women in developing countries, together with women of 'color,' have argued that much of the feminist literature emerges from the privileged women who live at the centre, whose perspective of reality excludes any knowledge or awareness of the lives of the women who live in developing countries or on the margin. They have challenged the universal notion of woman and have underlined the division among women.

The entries in the section on method and theory, "Methodological Considerations," take cognizance of this debate and its developments and aim to provide a guideline for understanding the complexity of women's work in developing countries. We turn to complementary and much more interactive techniques of data gathering by combining qualitative and quantitative methods. The entries provide a unique theoretical and methodological approach in order to grasp the multi-dimensional nature of women's work.

"Gender at Work" documents the sex segregation of work in developing countries as a whole. The entries show that studies of the labour force present only a partial view of women's segregated labour. This section describes women's work at home, in the paid labour market, in the tribal areas, in the rural settings and in the informal markets. The entries show that the home and market continually interact within the context of patriarchy and capitalism. The dialectic of gender relations interacts with that of race and class.

The issue, "Working for Change," which will be discussed later more in detail, is one of the major themes of this book. This section shows that, despite problems, various agencies and women themselves are at work to put women's issues on the top of the agenda.

The introductory chapter is followed by specific chapters on Africa, Asia, Latin America, the Caribbean and the Middle East. Each chapter starts with an Introduction which provides a background for understanding the issues which affect women's working lives in specific parts of the world. This general information makes it very clear that, for instance, women of Africa are affected by different sets of historical, political, social and cultural factors than women in Latin America. This background information makes the important point that women's working lives cannot be understood in isolation from the larger issues which characterise a particular society.

The second component of each chapter is the "Social Construction of Gender," which demonstrates the power of ideology in shaping women's lives. We use ideology in a broad sense to denote sets of beliefs concerning social, political and cultural issues which, together, construct our notion of 'woman' and legitimize women's subordinate position in society. Of importance is the construction of a subjective identity through the media, the state and the educational system, offering women images of values of the home, motherhood and paid work, which, like the system of social reproduction, vary between class and race. The variations in the role and forms of ideological apparatuses point to an important theme of this book, namely the contingency of ideologies.

The section on "Women, State and Development Policies," shows that the prevailing theories of social and political change in developing countries, represented by the poles of 'modernization' and 'dependency theory,' with many variations in between, have been subjected to substantial empirical and theoretical criticisms since their origin in the 1960s. More recently, the most penetrating challenge has come from feminist scholars. Modernization theory is criticized either for ignoring the sexual dimension of social change in the developing countries, or for simply asserting that economic modernization would liberate women. It has been argued that state policies of modernization and development in developing countries, by and large, have marginalized women, and have deprived them of their control over the resources and authority within the household, without lightening the heavy burden of their responsibilities.

The pivotal role of familial obligations in shaping women's working lives is the topic of the next section, "Work and Family." Women's participation in the world of paid work and their representation within it cannot be understood in isolation from their position in kinship and family structures and their relationship to childbearing and reproduction in the household. Women's position in the paid labour market is closely tied to their unpaid labour in the family. Women's unpaid labour continues to have a crucial effect on their identity as waged workers, in spite of their integral role within the paid labour force. The entries here question the separation between the public and private lives of women. They show that women's working lives can only be understood within its close connection to their family life.

This leads to a much debated discussion of women's experience in the labour market in "Women's Experience of Wage-Work." The entries strongly support the findings in the introductory chapter that the labour market is not a gender-neutral context to which women simply bring a set of preconditioned attitudes, but is permeated by implicit gender ideology activated through the practices of state, family, management and workers, including women themselves. Women participate in the labour market on a very different basis than men. Women's employment in the developing countries, much like their counterparts in the industrialized world, is in a limited range of occupations, and vertically, at the bottom of the occupational ladder. Such segregation corresponds with lower earnings and inferior working conditions for women and is accompanied by a division of labour within the home which accords women the major share of the domestic tasks.

The section, "Working in the Rural Areas," widely documents that the majority of women in Africa, Asia, Latin America, the Caribbean, and the Middle East depend on the land for their survival. They are the world's farmers and are largely responsible for the production of food: they grow the crops, gather the firewood, tend the animals, and bring in the water. Women in most of the rural areas are the main producers--growing food not only for their families, but also for sale. Women's participation in the production of food is an arduous and neglected area.

What emerges very clearly from the whole discussion on women's work is the multidimensional nature of their activities. Women are active in the family, in the national and international economy, in the community and are major contributors to craft and domestic production. They are present in both the paid and unpaid labour markets and in the formal and informal sectors of the economy. Moreover, survival of the rural economy and production of food in the developing countries rely on women. However, much of women's work, as the entries in this book show, remains invisible.

This book, as a whole, brings to the reader a sense of the difficulties that women face. However, the entries in section five, "Working for Change," provide evidence that significant changes can and do occur. This chapter raises important questions regarding the portrayal of women in developing countries as passive and as victims of a patriarchal ideology. One of the most remarkable themes emerging from this research is the strength of forces which are at work to improve women's situation. On the positive side, state and international institutions have become more aware of gender issues. Women themselves, individually and in groups, are attempting to change their lives. Women try to empower other women, they oppose their traditional roles, resist patriarchal authority and enter into negotiations both in the family and at work. As the Appendix on organisations and research centres demonstrates, women's issues are being addressed at many levels and in many places.

"Audiovisual Resources" provides further information for understanding women's lives. The general section in this chapter includes entries relevant to all developing countries. Audiovisual materials related to a specific area--Africa, Asia, Latin America, the Caribbean or the Middle East--are listed separately. Films and videos are listed by their titles, in alphabetical order. Finally, there are three separate indexes by author, country and region, and subject, which provide easy access to the entries in this book.

Acknowledgements

Special thanks go to George Butler, Dan Chekki, Arash Ghorayshi, Jane Lerner, Darlene Mann, Laureen Narfason, and Dana Sawchuck; each, in their own ways, made this book possible. I would like to express my appreciation to the Social Sciences and Humanities Research Council of Canada for providing the financial support for this book.

Chapter One

General Works

1.1 The Developing World and the Global Economy: An Introduction

1.   Adams, Nassau. Worlds Apart: The North-South Divide and the International System. London: Zed Books, 1993.

The author looks at the widening gaps between industrialized countries of the North and Third World countries of the South. In this major study of economic history, the author considers the international economic system as a significant factor in this division. This book helps us to understand one of the major problems of today's world economy. *(See 14, 15, 18, 26, 572)*.

2.   Afshar, Haleh (ed.). Women: Development and Survival in the Third World. London: Longman, 1991.

The authors show how women still have to struggle in order to gain access to the formal levels of policy making. In order to succeed in this struggle, it is important that women's work and contributions to the economy be recognized and acknowledged. This book aims to help achieve this goal. *(See 19, 22, 28, 72, 114, 278, 413, 453, 563, 570)*.

3.   Ahmed, Iftekhar (ed.). Technology and Rural Women: Conceptual and Empirical Issues. London: George Allen and Unwin, 1985.

This collection looks at the impact of technological change on women producers in rural areas, draws attention to sexual inequality and shows how technological change worsens women's position. Women's income in the household declines as they undergo the process of modernization. This study challenges the traditional approach to modernization and development. *(See 176, 306, 340, 578).*

4.   Danforth, Sandra. "Women, Development, and Public Policy: A Selected Bibliography." Women and Politics 2, no. 4 (Winter 1982): 107-24.

This bibliography includes selected published academic literature in English since 1960 on women in the developing world, with an emphasis on public policy. *(See 28).*

5.   Dankelman, Irene and Joan Davidson. Women and Environment in the Third World: Alliance for the Future. London: Earthscan Publications Limited, 1988.

This book presents a clear account of the problems that women face in the management of basic resources. The authors look at the lack of response from international organizations and offer ways that women can organize to meet environmental, social and economic challenges. *(See 21, 283).*

6.   Frank, Andre Gunder. Crisis: In the Third World. New York: Holmes and Meier Publishers, 1981.

The author, a leading scholar on Third World studies, offers a powerful perspective on the political, economic, and social dimensions of the world situation today. He focuses on the Third World and the ways Third World countries affect and are being affected by the powerful forces of the global economy. *(See 22, 69, 370, 558).*

7.   Frobel, F.; J. Heinrichs and O. Kreye. The New International Division of Labour: Structural Unemployment in Industrialized Countries and Industrialization in

Developing Countries. Cambridge: Cambridge University Press, 1980.

This book shows the change in the international division of labour and how a large section of industrial production has been transferred to Third World and Eastern European countries where labour is cheap. It provides a clear analysis of the growth of the free zones in the developing countries and sheds light on our knowledge of the growing inter-relationship between the Third World and industrialized countries. *(See 1, 137, 412)*.

8.   Gugler, Josef (ed.). The Urbanization of the Third World. Oxford: Oxford University Press, 1988.

The collection in this book provides a comprehensive account of urbanization in the Third World and looks at the relationship between the rural and urban sectors. It also investigates the relationship between urban migration and urban labour market. *(See 10, 178, 296, 391, 419)*.

9.   Hall, Stuart and Bram Giebon (eds.). Formations of Modernity. London: Polity Press, 1992.

This book provides an account of the important historical processes, institutions and ideas that have shaped the development of modern societies. It critically examines the roots of modern knowledge and its impact on the emerging identity of the 'West' through its relation and construction of 'other civilization'. *(See 31, 62)*.

10.   Harvet, Jose (ed.). Staying on: Retention and Migration in Peasant Societies. Ottawa: University of Ottawa Press, 1988.

Third World countries are facing growing urbanization. The author systematically addresses the critical issues that urbanization creates in developing countries and looks at divergent views on this issue. By focusing on a number of case studies, this book addresses key questions facing developing countries. *(See 8, 196,*

237, 611).

11.   Heisey, D. Ray. "The Role of Asian women in National
       Development Efforts."   Women's Studies International
       Forum 6, no. 1 (1983): 85-96.

       Discusses the origin and function of the Asian Women's
institute.   Looks at nine women's study centres in Iran, India,
Pakistan, Korea, Lebanon, and Japan.   Shows that the joint
projects across national boundaries are making an impact. *(See 60,
246, 428).*

12.   Joekes, Susan P. (ed.). Women in the World Economy: an
       INSTRAW Study. Toronto: Oxford university Press, 1987.

       The author looks at the impact of the international economy
on women in developing countries. She examines the issues from
the perspective of women in paid and unpaid work and analyses
women's employment trends by geographical region and sector of
the economy. *(See 27, 29, 410, 566, 684).*

13.   Johnson, Stanley P. World Population and the United
       Nations: Challenge and Response. Cambridge: Cambridge
       University Press, 1987.

       This publication looks at the unprecedented growth of the
world population and the challenges that it poses to the United
Nations and its system of agencies. A substantial part of the book
discusses the United Nations's achievements regarding population
issues. *(See 17, 159, 186, 396, 565).*

14.   Kemp, Tom. Industrialization in the Non-Western World.
       London: Longman, 1989.

       This book focuses on a series of case studies from Japan,
the Soviet Union, India, China, Brazil and Nigeria. It shows that
the experience of industrialization for these countries has been very
different from the capitalist West. It also provides important
insights which help readers to understand major changes in the

economic trends in recent years. *(See 22).*

15. Latouche, Serge. The End of the Affluent Society?: An Exploration of Post-Development. London: Zed Books, 1993.

A critical analysis of the process of global modernization in a Western ideological mould. The author argues that this model of development does not fit the Third World's needs. However, he finds hope in the response of the people of the Third World in respect to preserving their own cultures. *(See 1, 26, 559).*

16. Loewenson, Rene. Modern Plantation Agriculture: Corporate Wealth and Labour Squalor. London: Zed Books, 1992.

The author focuses on Zimbabwe and examines plantation agriculture in various parts of the Third World. This book shows the centrality of large-scale agricultural production in the Third World countries, but demonstrates the cost to the real producers-- the farm labourers. *(See 24, 159, 555, 564, 668).*

17. Martin, Michael and Terry R. Kandal (eds.). Studies of Development and Change in the Modern World. Oxford: Oxford University Press, 1989.

This book examines the theoretical and methodological issues crucial to the study of development and social change. It uses case studies to illustrate the importance of the link between the core and the peripheral societies in the world system and shows how such a perspective will aid to evaluate the major national and regional issues. *(See 6, 24, 64, 67, 576).*

18. McCormick, Brian Joseph. The World Economy: Patterns of Growth and Change. Oxford: Philip Allan Publishers, 1988.

This book goes beyond the traditional economic textbooks and discusses world trading relations. It analyses in detail the linkages of the global economy. *(See 1, 17, 23, 398, 572)*.

19.   Mies, Maria. Patriarchy and Accumulation on a World
       Scale: Women in the International Division of Labour.
       London: Zed books, 1987.

The author argues that the main challenge facing feminism
is to understand that patriarchy and accumulation on a world Scale
constitute the structural and ideological framework within which
women's reality operates. She looks at the origin of the gender
division of labour and calls for the development of a feminist
perspective for liberating women. *(See 2, 27, 29, 73, 99, 137,
271, 401)*.

20.   Peterson, Spike V. (ed.). Gendered States: Feminist (Re)
       Visions of International Relations Theory. Boulder: Lynne
       Rienner Publishers, 1992.

Feminists in this collection rewrite the central concepts in
political and international theory--the state, power and sovereignty.
The authors provide a new direction for international relations.
(See 6, 17, 29, 277).

21.   Rao, Arura. Women's Studies International: Nairobi and
       Beyond. New York: Feminist Press at the City University
       of New York, 1991.

Based on Women's Studies International workshops held at
the Nairobi NGO united Nations Forum, this book contains essays
from around the world which deal with gender issues and the links
with government policy, development project, education and
research. It provides, also, an elaborate section on women's
programs in various part of the world. *(See 567)*.

22.   Rodda, Annabel. Women and the Environment. London:
       Zed Books, 1991.

The author argues that the deterioration of the earth's
environment is having an impact on all its inhabitants. For women

worldwide, however, it has a particular significance. This book examines all the major environmental issues, but focuses on women's roles as users, producers and managers, and shows how environmental deterioration affects women's health. This book could serve as a guide to education and action, and also provides a bibliography and a list of relevant organizations. *(See 5, 283)*.

23.   Simpson, Edward S. The Developing World: An Introduction. New York: Longman, 1987.

This book examines theories of development and uses case studies to address the fundamental issues of development in a part of the world alternately described as the Third World, the South and the developing world. The author identifies the major issues in various developing countries. *(See 6, 14, 576)*.

24.   Singer, Hans W. and Javed A. Ansari. Rich and Poor Countries: Consequences of International Disorder. London: Unwin Hyman, 1988.

This book focuses on key international issues and uses factual analysis to show the fundamental relationships between the rich and poor countries. New material points to the emergence of a new international environment in which the situation of poor countries has worsened. *(See 1, 18, 22, 561, 575)*.

25.   Sobhan, Rehman. Agrarian Reform and Social Transformation: Preconditions for Development. London: Zed books, 1993.

The author provides a powerful critical look at the traditional policies on land reform. He presents a comparative survey of the historical experiences of land reform in the Third World and argues that land reform should be put on the top of the development agenda and should be understood in its political, social and economic complexity. *(See 16, 388, 426, 616)*.

26.   The South Centre. Whose Brave New World? Prospects for the South. (Foreword by Julius K. Nyerere). The South Centre, 1993.

This publication describes the changes in the world system, including the challenges facing countries in the South and the current sources of instability. It provides an alternative vision of world development. *(See 27, 402, 557, 560).*

27.   Sparr, Pamela (ed.). Mortgaging Women's Lives: Feminist Critiques of Structural Adjustment. London: Zed Books, 1993.

The collection in this book looks at the adverse impact of the World Bank's structural adjustment program on women. It employs examples from various countries to provide evidence for its claims. A very timely study which helps to rethink IMF and World Bank policies. *(See 1, 23, 77, 402, 569).*

28.   Staudt, Kathleen A. and Jane S. Jaquette (eds.). Women in Developing Countries: A Policy Focus. New York: The Haworth Press, 1983.

The selections in this collection show that development, whether in capitalist or socialist economies, continues to marginalize women. The contributions in this book reflect a new phase in women and development. This book reminds us that women's subordination remains the key to theory and practice in development. *(See 2, 113, 570).*

29.   Sylvester, Christine (Guest editor). Alternatives: Social Transformation and Human Governance; Feminists Write International Relations. (Special Journal Issue), 1993.

This special issue of Alternatives is devoted to international relations from a feminist point of view. It brings in a variety of voices which are normally excluded from the discussion of international relations. *(See 27, 31, 141).*

30.   Szentes, Tamas. The Transformation of the World Economy: New Directions and New Interests. London: Zed Books, 1988.

This comprehensive survey explores the nature of the world's capitalist economy and its increasing tendency toward internationalization. This tendency will enhance the gap between developed and developing countries, to which the author draws the attention of the reader. *(See 1, 7, 573)*.

31.   Wallerstein, Immanuel. Unthinking Social Science: The Limits of Nineteenth Century Paradigms. Cambridge: Polity Press, 1991.

The author, a leading scholar of Third World studies, argues that we have to 'unthink' many of the presumptions which still remain the foundation of dominant perspectives today. For instance, once considered a liberating factor for nations regarding 'development', they have become a barrier to a clear understanding of the modern social world. This book helps to understand the evolution of Wallerstein's thought. *(See 6, 9, 27)*.

1.2 Understanding Women's Work: Theoretical Considerations

1.2.1 Feminist Theory

32.   Anderson, Margaret L. Race, Class and Gender: An Anthology. Scarborough: Nelson Canada, 1992.

This collection examines race, class and gender from a sociological perspective. It shows the importance of these experiences for women's lives, both as individuals and within groups. *(See 33, 34)*.

33.   Basow, Susan A. Gender Stereotypes. Scarborough: Nelson Canada, 1992.

This third edition provides an interdisciplinary approach to understanding sex-role stereotypes. It shows how stereotypes affect women and how they are maintained. *(See 32, 34, 50, 52, 252, 475)*.

34.   Britain, Arthur and Mary Maynard. Sexism, Racism and
       Oppression. Oxford: Basil Blackwell, 1984.

The authors criticize various theoretical perspectives for
their inability to explain the roots of sexism and racism. They
demonstrate the need to break away from deterministic approaches
and offer an alternative which emphasizes the importance of
everyday activities in the reproduction of oppression. *(See 32, 33)*.

35.   Connelly, Patricia. "On Marxism and Feminism." Studies
       in Political Economy 12 (Fall 1983): 153-161.

Provides a review of the debate between feminist and
Marxist writers regarding the issues of gender and class.
Concludes that a Marxist framework is very useful, but that we
need new categories and concepts to understand women's
oppression. A very important piece for understanding the debate
among feminist theorists. *(See 40)*.

36.   England, Paula. Theory on Gender/Feminism on Theory.
       New York: Aldine de Gruyter, 1993.

This collection of original essays presents a critical
evaluation of various theoretical perspectives on gender inequality.
A must reading for those interested in the existing debate on
women's status in society. *(See 35, 47, 49)*.

37.   Fay, Brian. Critical Social Science: Liberation and its
       Limits. Ithaca: Cornell University Press, 1987.

The author presents and assesses the foundation of critical
social science. He evaluates the metaphysical, ethical and political
assumptions that underpin this vision and asserts that it provides a
one-sided picture of human life. An attempt is made to explore
ideas such as empowerment, emancipation, liberation and
autonomy. *(See 39)*.

38.   Ferguson, Ann. Sexual Democracy: Women, Oppression
       and Revolution. Oxford: Westview Press, 1991.

The author provides a critical analysis of feminist theory and develops a new theory of domination. She defends a multi-system approach encompassing the overlapping interactions of sex, race and class. *(See 36).*

39.   Fox Keller, Evelyn. Reflections on Gender and Science. New Haven: Yale University Press, 1985.

Through this collection, the author addresses the relationship between gender and science. The essays are premised on the recognition that both gender and science are socially constructed categories. *(See 40, 42).*

40.   Gunew, Sneja (ed.). A Reader in Feminist Knowledge. London: Routledge, 1990.

This anthology takes into account various differences among women and presents recent major writings in feminism. It looks at. feminism and postmodernism, post structuralism, new spirituality and other issues of central importance to women's studies. *(See 41, 42, 46).*

41.   Hawkesworth, M. E. Beyond Oppression: Feminist Theory and Political Strategy. New York: Continuum, 1990.

This book argues that feminism and social justice are linked and aims to analyze concepts central to the construction of masculinity and femininity. It discusses theoretical perspectives regarding women's inequality and provides strategies for moving beyond gender oppression. *(See 46).*

42.   Hill Collins, Patricia. Black Feminist Thought: Knowledge, Consciousness, and the Politics of Empowerment. New York: Routledge, 1990.

The author combines theory and feminist practice by sharing with readers the voices of other African-American women. This book examines familiar themes related to women and challenges white feminist dominance of feminist theory. *(See 43,*

44, 54, 55, 80).

43.   Hirsch, Marianne and Evelyn Fox Keller (eds.). Conflicts
       in Feminism. New York: Routledge, 1990.

This book provides a broad narrative of women's history
and feminist theory. It discusses feminists' concerns with major
institutional structures and focuses on contested sites within
feminism. *(See 46, 61, 70, 172, 601).*

44.   Hooks, Bell. Talking Back: Thinking Feminist, Thinking
       Black. Toronto: Between The Lines, 1989.

This collection of 25 articles makes a powerful presentation
by women of 'colour' who have traditionally been oppressed and
silenced. They emphasize the need to talk back. *(See 42, 74,
143).*

45.   Jagger, Alison and Paula S. Rothenberg (eds.). Feminist
       Frameworks: Alternative Theoretical Accounts of the
       Relations Between Women and Men. New York: McGraw-
       Hill Book Company, 1984.

This selection provides a unique approach to the material on
feminism and shows that feminism is not monolithic. It helps
readers understand how and why different theories of feminism
explain gender relations. *(See 40).*

46.   Joseph, Gloria I. and Jill Lewis (eds.). Common
       Differences: Conflicts in Black and White Feminist
       Perspectives. Boston: South End Press, 1986.

This book brings together a number of important
contributions and addresses the differences between black and
white women's perspectives, attitudes and concerns. It discusses
vital issues where there are important differences among feminists.
(See 42, 43, 71).

47.   Lowe, Marian and Ruth Hubbard (eds.). Woman's Nature:

Rationalizations of Inequality. New York: Pergamon Press, 1983.

This collection of essays is about false descriptions of women's nature and about how such myths serve to limit women's participation in society, distort women's views of themselves and constrain their work and future. *(See 36, 475).*

48.   McDowell, Lindand and Rosemary Pringle. Defining Women: Social Institutions and Gender Divisions. Cambridge: Polity Press, 1992.

This book offers a detailed analysis of the social, economic and political positions of women in society and how social institutions construct gender. It addresses the question of differences between women and men and among women themselves, and poses a challenge to the universal notion of woman. *(See 40).*

49.   Nicholson, Linda J. (ed.). Feminism/Postmodernism. New York: Routledge, 1990.

This collection of articles addresses the benefits and dangers of postmodernism for feminist theory. This edition, as a whole, brings out the major tensions between modernist and postmodernist theories of women. *(See 36).*

50.   Okin, Susan Moller. Women in Western Political Thought. New Jersey: Princeton University Press, 1979.

This scholarly study provides a sharp criticism of basic notions in Western political thought. Although women have obtained the formal right of citizenship, they remain second-class citizens. The author turns to the tradition of political philosophy to investigate the roots of gendered ideology. *(See 33, 57, 81).*

51.   Reinharz, Shulamit, Marti Bombyk, and Janet Wright. "Methodological Issues in Feminist Research: A Bibliography of Literature in Women's Studies, Sociology

and Psychology." Women's Studies International Forum 6, no. 4 (1983): 437-54.

This bibliography provides an easy access to the rich and varied literature on feminist concerns. The references are drawn from psychological and sociological research and from the research in women's studies. It focuses on the literature published in the United States, but is very useful for those who want to familiarize themselves with the academic literature relevant to feminist research.

52.   Roos, Patricia A. Gender and Work: A Comparative Analysis of Industrial Societies. New York: State University of New York, 1985.

This book is based on an analysis of 12 industrialized countries and shows a consistent pattern of occupational sex-segregation which reflects structural features common to all modern industrialized countries. This is a milestone study on sex and marital differences in employment, occupation and earning capacity. *(See 33)*.

53.   Ruth, Sheila (ed.). Issues in Feminism: An Introduction to Women's Studies. Mountain View: Mayfield Publishing Co., 1990.

The author brings together a varied selection of classic and contemporary works from various disciplines on women. She addresses differences in class, ethnicity and sexual orientation. *(See 52)*.

54.   Scarborough, Cathy. "Conceptualizing Black Women's Employment Experiences." Yale Law Journal 98, no. 7 (May 1989): 1457-78.

The author provides a historical account of how the law has perceived and treated Black women, examining the experience of Black women in America from slavery to the present. Argues that Black women's experience cannot be understood as reflecting a combination of Black men's and white women's experiences. *(See 42, 439)*

55.   Spelman, Elizabeth V. <u>Inessential Woman: Problems of Exclusion in Feminist Thought</u>. London: The Women's Press Ltd., 1990.

A powerful argument against white middle class bias in feminist thought. This book argues that women come from all classes, races, ages and religions, and questions assumptions of homogeneity among women in feminist theory. A passionate argument for widening the scope of feminist theory to include women from various walks of life. *(See 42, 57, 59)*.

56.   Stacey, Judith. "Sexism by a Subtler Name: Postindustrial Conditions and Postfeminist Consciousness." <u>Socialist Review</u> 96, vol. 17, no. 6 (November-December 1987): 7-30.

Judith Stacey explores the links between the recent transition to the "postindustrial" stage of capitalist development and the rise and decline of radical feminism in the U.S. She uses the concept of "postfeminism" to describe her research findings on family life in California's "Silicon Valley."

57.   Sydie, R. A. <u>Natural Women, Cultured Men: A Feminist Perspective on Sociological Theory</u>. Toronto: Methuen, 1987.

This book examines classical social theorists from a feminist perspective. It shows that, in general, sociological thinking is characterized by a dichotomized and hierarchical view of sex relationships. *(See 50, 59, 81)*.

58.   Unger, Rhoda K. (ed.). <u>Representations: Social Constructions of Gender</u>. New York: Baywood Publishing Co., 1989.

This edited book provides a collection of stories about

women--about the conflicts, choices and opportunities that are present in women's lives. *(See 55, 562).*

59.   Wallace, Ruth A. (ed.).   Feminism and Sociological Theory. London: Sage Publications, 1989.

This book provides an overview of achievements by feminist scholarship, but shows that the canon of the social science is unaware of this scholarship. It offers an attempt to bring feminism back to the forefront of theoretical thinking. *(See 50, 57).*

1.2.2 Feminism: Voices from the Developing Countries

60.   Allen, Josephine A. V. "Women as a Major Force in the Planning and Implementation of Social Development Strategies." Social Development Issues 9, no. 1 (Spring 1985): 34-52.

Examines the barriers that limit women's achievement in economic development. The author argues that the existing emphasis of development projects on technical aspects of development must give way to increased concern for human capital. There is a need to involve women in the design and implementation of development projects. *(See 11, 428).*

61.   Badran, Margot and Miriam Cooke. Opening the Gates: A Century of Arab Feminist Writing. Bloomington: Indiana University Press, 1990.

This anthology of short stories, poems, tales, memoirs, articles and speeches is the first collection of Arab women's feminist writings. It reveals the range of feminist expressions over a century and shows that feminist discourse existed in the Arab world before there was an explicit term for feminism. *(See 43, 550).*

62.   Baykan, Aysegul. "Women between Fundamentalism and Modernity." in Bryan S. Turner ed., Theories of Modernity

and Postmodernity. London: Sage Publications, 1990.

This article addresses the issues related to social transformation, global political movements, and the place and right of women in society. Shows that it would be a mistake, both theoretically and methodologically, to take beliefs and practices in Middle Eastern societies as a continuation of historically-fixed traditions and culture. *(See 9, 79, 481)*.

63.   Bourne, Jenny.   "Homelands of the Mind: Jewish Feminism and Identity Politics." Race and Class 29, no. 1 (Summer 1987): 1-24.

Uses the dilemmas which face Jewish women and makes a strong case against a feminism which is separatist, individualistic and inward-looking. Provides a critical and enlightening look at Jewish feminism. *(See 43, 477)*.

64.   Dube, S.C. Modernization and Development: The Search for Alternative Paradigms. London: Zed Books, 1988.

The author critically evaluates various theories of development and argues for an alternative theory of development. This alternative model, the author argues, can no longer take the narrow goal of economic growth as its primary objective. *(See 9, 17, 76)*.

65.   Haddad, Yvonne Y. "Islam, Women and Revolution in Twentieth-Century Arab Thought." The Muslim World LXXIV, nos. 3-4 (July-October 1984): 137-161.

Twentieth-century Arab thought has been dominated by three ideologies: the nationalist, the socialist, and the Islamist. Discusses the position of women within each of these ideologies and delineates the characteristics that distinguish the Arab feminist movement from its counterpart in the West. It concludes that Arab women have been modernized, revolutionized, and Islamized. Women have been defined to fit a range of symbolic categories appropriate to the current system. *(See 61)*.

66.   Haggis, Jane. "The Feminist Research Process: Defining a Topic." Studies in Sexual Politics 16 (1987): 23-37.

Criticizes Western social science for being exclusionary. Combines the critique of colonialism with feminist theory to study women in India as a project for a Ph.D. *(See 55).*

67.   Hale, Sylvia M. "Integrating Women in Development Models and Theories." Atlantis 11, no. 1 (Fall 1985): 45-63.

Criticizes the prevailing theories of development for their lack of consideration of women and emphasizes the need for a new approach which would be more appropriate to their situation. Concludes that it is essential to focus on economic development for women as the basis for all other social change. *(See 17, 27).*

68.   Hatem, Mervat. "Class and Patriarchy as Competing Paradigms for the Study of Middle Eastern Women." Comparative Studies in Society and History 29, no. 4 (October 1987): 811-818.

Provides a general review of various writings on Middle Eastern women. Recognizes the contribution of the Marxian approach, but is very critical of it and calls for an alternative framework. *(See 61, 482).*

69.   Kay, Cristobal. Latin American Theories of Development and Underdevelopment. London: Routledge, 1989.

A systematic and comprehensive study of theories of development and underdevelopment. The author critically evaluates various theories of underdevelopment and argues that in the developed world there has been a tendency to rely on partial knowledge of dependency theory. *(See 6).*

70.   Lazreg, Marnia. "Feminism and Difference: The Perils of Writing as a Woman on Women in Algeria." Feminist Issues 14, no. 1 (Spring 1988): 81-107.

The author acknowledges the potential of feminism for liberation, but is critical of Western feminism. It is argued that Algerian feminists are caught between three overlapping discourses, namely: the male discourse on gender difference, social science discourse on the people of Africa and the Middle East, and academic discourse on women from the same societies. *(See 43)*.

71.   Mohanty, Chandra Talpade; Ann Russo and Lourdes Torres (eds.). Third World Women and the Politics of Feminism. Bloomington: Indiana university Press, 1991.

This book challenges Euro-American feminism as well as male-dominated narratives on Third World women. It traces Third World women's engagement with feminism in the contexts of decolonization, nationalism and corporate capitalism. *(See 46, 601)*.

72.   Nader, Laura. "Orientalism, Occidentalism and the Control of Women." Cultural Dynamics 2, no. 3 (1989): 323-355.

Uses Edward Said and Antonio Gramsci to develop a framework to identify how images of women in other societies can be prejudicial to women in one's own society. Discusses the ways in which images of gender relationships fit into the Western views of the Muslim world or how the Arab Muslim world constructs visions of the West. *(See 2, 75, 479)*.

73.   Ong, Aihwa. Spirits of Resistance and Capitalist Discipline: Factory Women in Malaysia. Albany: State University of New York Press, 1987.

Argues that capitalist development in Malaysia entails new forms of discipline in the everyday life of Malays, who, up to recently, were largely rooted in village life and engaged in small-scale cash cropping. Explores how changing relationships in the peasant household, village, and global factory mediate divergent attitudes towards work and sexuality among Malays and within the wider society. *(See 19, 239, 251, 273)*.

74.   Patterson, T.   "Out of Egypt: A Talk with Nawal El
        Saadawi."   With A. Gilliam.   Freedomways, Special
        Middle East Issue 23 (1983): 3.

        The author interviews Nawal El Saadawi, an Egyptian
psychiatrist, scholar, novelist and feminist.   It focuses on
Saadawi's views on Western feminism and women of the Third
World in general. *(See 44, 484).*

75.   Said, Edward W.   Orientalism: Western Concepts of the
        Orient.   Harmond Worth: Penguin, 1985.

        The author analyzes the various discourses and institutions
which constructed and produced as an object of knowledge, that
entity called the 'orient'.   Said calls this discourse 'orientalism'.
(See 72, 479).

76.   Salmen, Lawrence F.   Listen to the People: Participant
        Observer Evaluation of Development Projects.   Oxford:
        Oxford University Press, 1987.

        The author draws from his experience of living among the
people and argues for a development project which takes the view
and needs of the ordinary people into account.   From this
perspective, the author critically evaluates the World Bank's
projects in Latin America. *(See 64, 141).*

77.   Scott, Alison MacEwen.   "Women and Industrialisation:
        Examining the 'Female Marginalisation' Thesis."   Journal
        of Development Studies 22, no. 4 (July 1986): 649-80.

        This study is concerned with the usefulness of the
marginalization thesis in explaining the impact of capitalist
industrialization on women's economic position.   It argues that
there are substantial theoretical and methodological problems with
the female marginalization thesis in developing countries. The two
case studies in this paper show that while women may be
marginalized from some forms of employment, they are selectively
incorporated into others. *(See 26).*

78.   Sen, Gita with Caren Crown. Development, Crisis, and Alternative Visions: Third World Women's Perspectives. Olden: A.S. Verbum, 1985.

An ever growing group of activists who are committed to the search for alternative and more equitable development processes has launched DAWN. This book is an integral part of the process. It aims at synthesizing women's experience with development, and pays particular attention to the impact of the global economy and its crisis on women. *(See 22, 77, 176).*

79.   Shaheed, Farida. "The Cultural Articulation of Patriarchy: Legal Systems, Islam and Women." South Asia Bulletin 6, no. 1 (Spring 1986): 38-44.

There are similarities between the patriarchal system in Pakistan and that in the West, but in Pakistan this system acquires specific characteristics. The author shows the extent to which patriarchal ideology has been justified by invoking the Islamic belief system. *(See 62).*

80.   Steady, Filomina Chioma (ed.). The Black Woman Cross-Culturally. Cambridge: Schenkman Publishing Co., 1981.

This anthology brings together, for the first time in a cross-cultural perspective, a body of previously fragmented literature on black women. It discusses common themes and synthesizes the growing literature on the subject. The literature used in this book is representative of the black women in Africa, the Caribbean, South America and the U.S. *(See 42).*

81.   Tillion, Germaine. The Republic of Cousins. (Translated by Quintin Hoare). London: Zed Press, 1983.

In the fifth edition of this book, the author argues that women's oppression is not an aberration specific to Islam, but part of a legacy from pagan prehistory that weighs upon Christian and Muslim alike. *(See 50, 57).*

1.3 Understanding Women's Work: Methodological Considerations

82.   Armstrong, Pat, and Hugh Armstrong. "Beyond Numbers:
        Problems with Quantitative Data." Alternate Routes 6
        (1983): 1-40.

        The authors use insights from their interviews to show the
limits of the quantitative method of data collection employed by
Statistics Canada. Qualitative data is needed to remedy the existing
deficiencies in data collection, especially regarding women. *(See
103, 110, 111)*.

83.   Armstrong, Pat and Hugh Armstrong. Theorizing
        Women's Work. Toronto: Garamond Press, 1990.

        The authors look at the nature of women's work and how
it has been changing, showing the importance of both personal and
political in understanding women's work. They critically examine
the existing theories of women and work and demystify theories by
making the everyday life relevant. A very useful introduction to
theories of women and work. *(See 89, 109)*.

84.   Bertaux, Daniel and Martin Kohli. "The Life Story
        Approach: A Continental View." Annual Review of
        Sociology 10 (1984): 215-237.

        There is a revival of sociological interest in the use of life
stories. This paper provides a survey of this important trend in a
number of countries: the U.S., Poland, Germany, Italy, France,
Spain, and Britain. Life story method is tied to a variety of
disciplines   and   theoretical   approaches   and   has   deep
multidisciplinary roots. *(See 87, 88, 105, 140)*.

85.   Bozzoli, Belinda. "Migrant Women and South African
        Social Change: Biographical Approaches to Social
        Analysis." African Studies 44, no. 1 (1985): 87-96.

        This paper relies on the Oral Documentation Project and
discusses the advantages and pitfalls of the biographical approach

to social analysis. Points to the aims and ideals of using individual biographies and stresses the importance of the concern for representativeness of individual cases. *(See 155).*

86.   Briggs, Charles L. "Questions for the Ethnographer: A Critical Examination of the Role of the Interview in Fieldwork." Semiotica 46, nos. 2-4 (1983): 233-61.

The author uses his fieldwork experience to present the limits of interviewing as a meta-communicative tool in ethnography and stresses the following in ethnographic research: 1) basic understanding of the communicative norms, 2) periodic checks on the effectiveness of one's interviews, and 3) emphasizing the meta-communicative events that are used by members of society. *(See 91, 112).*

87.   Bytheway, W. R. "Beginning with Life Histories: Interviewing in the Families of Welsh Steelworkers." Current Perspectives on Aging and the Lifecycle 3 (1989): 119-125.

On the basis of interviews of steelworkers' families in Wales, the author provides important insights for grasping the experience of everyday life. *(See 84, 88, 105).*

88.   Camargo, Aspasia, Valentina da Rocha-Lima, and Lucia Hippolito. "The Life History Approach in Latin America." Life Stories 1 (1985): 41-54.

Discusses the anthropological roots of life history in Latin America, and reviews studies which have made use of this method in Brazil, Argentina, and Mexico. Concludes that in this complex region, life history can help us to understand life experience in Latin America. *(See 84, 87, 90, 105, 164).*

89.   Combessie, Jean-Claude. "A propos de methodes: effets d'optique, heuristique et objectivation." BMS, Bulletin de Methodologie Sociologique 10 (Avril 1986): 4-24.

This case study of a rural area in Spain makes the important argument that qualitative and quantitative methods are complementary. By using both approaches, the researcher is able to bring out the multiple dimensions of everyday life. *(See 83, 92)*

90.   Davison, Jean (with the women of Mutira). <u>Voices From Mutira: Lives of Rural Gikuyu Women</u>. Boulder: Lynne Rienner Publishers, 1989.

A very rich collection of life histories which tell us about Gikuyu women as farmers, wives and mothers. Women describe, in their own ways, how they view forces that affect their lives. *(See 84, 87)*.

91.   Dorsky, Susan. <u>Women of Amran: A Middle Eastern Ethnographic Study</u>. Salt Lake City: University of Utah Press, 1986.

This study focuses on a small town in Yemen and describes the day-to-day realities of women's lives. It provides abundant case materials which challenge the traditional one-dimensional view of Arab women. *(See 86, 112)*.

92.   Durant-Gonzalez, Victoria. "Evolution of a Research Methodology." <u>Social and Economic Studies</u> 35, no. 2 (June 1986): 31-58.

This project employs multi-level methodology to increase knowledge about Caribbean women's participation in economic and social development at both the national and regional levels. It uses both qualitative and quantitative methods to grasp the diversity of expressions in women's everyday lives. *(See 89, 104, 350)*.

93.   Faulkner, Constance. "Women's Studies in the Muslim Middle East." <u>Journal of Ethnic Studies</u> 8, no. 3 (Fall 1980): 67-76.

The author points out that research on women in the Middle East is sparse, eclectic, idealized, and has theoretical and methodological problems. Stresses the need for an interdisciplinary approach in Middle Eastern studies. Reviews some of the most recent works utilizing effective methodology in studying women in the Middle East. *(See 100, 103).*

94.   Feldman, Elliot J. A Practical Guide to the Conduct of Field Research in the Social Sciences. Boulder: Westview Press, 1981.

The author offers a direct and clear guidance in defining problems for research, organizing and conducting a research project. He addresses the basic and central questions on the topic. *(See 97).*

95.   Glesne, Corrine and Alan Peshkin. Becoming Qualitative Researcher: An Introduction. White Plains: Longman, 1992.

This publication presents the reader with various stages of qualitative methodology; research design, pilot studies, interviewing techniques, use of theory, data analysis and report writing. *(See 94, 98).*

96.   Harvey, Lee. Critical Social Research. London: Unwin Hyman, 1990.

The author intends to bridge the gap between qualitative and quantitative research. His aim is to provide knowledge that challenges the oppressive social structures. Each section of this study addresses various forms of oppression--those based on class, gender and race. Through a variety of case studies, the author demonstrates the link between methodology and practical issues. *(See 95).*

97.   Jacknis, Ira. "Margaret Mead and Gregory Bateson in Bali: Their Use of Photography and Film." Cultural Anthropology 3, no. 2 (May 1988): 160-177.

An excellent review of Margaret Mead's corpus of visual

anthropology done in Bali during the 1930s. Photography was used by Mead's team as an important tool to present major theoretical findings in the field. *(See 94, 107).*

98.   Livings, Gail S. "Discovering the World of Twentieth Century Trade Union Waitresses in the West: A Nascent Analysis of Working Class Women's Meanings of Self and Work." Current Perspectives on Aging and the Life Cycle 3 (1989): 141-73.

This paper uses the method of oral history to understand the formation of consciousness among wage-earning women in a period of industrialization and expansion of women's paid employment. It discusses how these working women dealt with the conflict arising from their traditional role and their tasks in the paid labour force. *(See 95).*

99.   Ollenburger, Jane C. and Helen A. Moore. A Sociology of Women: The Intersection of Patriarchy, Capitalism and Colonization. New Jersey: Prentice Hall, 1992.

This book defines the sociology of women as a comprehensive perspective on the diversity of women's experiences of structured inequality. The authors integrate macro and micro sociological methods and are informed by feminist theory. *(See 19, 109, 492).*

100.   Pastner, Carroll. "Rethinking the Role of the Woman Field Worker in Purdah Societies." Human Organization 41, no. 3 (Fall 1982): 262-64.

The author discusses her experience of research in Pakistan and provides suggestions for foreign women field workers in societies characterized by purdah; that is, sexual segregation and the seclusion of women. *(See 93, 103).*

101.   Pirès, Alvaro P. "La méthode qualitative en Amérique du Nord: un débat manqué (1918-1960)." Sociologie et Sociétés 14, no. 1 (April 1982): 15-29.

The author looks at the historical development of sociology in North America to show why qualitative methodology has been abandoned. It is argued that the socioeconomic development has influenced the adoption of a quantitative method. However, in recent years qualitative method has been making a comeback. *(See 95)*.

102. Rassam, Amal. "Towards a Theoretical Framework for the Study of Women in the Arab World." Cultures 8, no. 3 (1982): 121-37.

The approach to the study of women in the Arab world has suffered from a "male bias" common in women's studies. In addition, most of those who study women in the Middle East avoid theoretical issues. Suggests that women's status can only be understood in terms of: the social organization of power; the ideological and institutional means of controlling women's sexuality; and the sexual division of labour in society. *(See 93, 100)*.

103. Recchini de Lattes, Zulma and Catalina H. Wainerman. "Unreliable Account of Women's Work: Evidence from Latin American Census Statistics." Signs 11, no. 4 (summer 1986): 740-750.

Takes examples from Latin American and Caribbean statistics to show that women's economic contributions in developing countries are either overlooked or underestimated. This is an international problem and is reinforced by the methods of data collection advised by the United Nations Statistical Commission. *(See 82)*.

104. Reinharz, Shulamit. Feminist Methods in Social Research. Oxford: Oxford University Press, 1992.

This book focuses on feminist methods and shows that a diversity of methods have been a great asset to feminist scholarship. It raises important questions about doing research. *(See 92)*.

105.   Robertson, Claire.   "In Pursuit of Life Histories: The
        Problem of Bias." Frontiers 7, no. 2 (1983): 63-69.

        Suggests that the collection of life histories should be
conducted with extreme care. Identifies a number of biases that
one may face using the method of life history. *(See 87, 88).*

106.   Robinson, Beverly J. "Life Narratives: A Structural Model
        for the Study of Black Women's Culture." Current
        Perspectives on Aging and the Life Cycle 3 (1989): 127-40.

        The author uses narratives and oral history to study older
black American women. It is argued that this method allows
women to define themselves. Life narrative is an important tool
which moves away from myopic analysis to a well-rounded view
of social life. *(See 54, 87, 88, 105).*

107.   Schwartz, Dona. "Visual Ethnography: Using Photography
        in Qualitative Research." Qualitative Sociology 12, no. 2
        (Summer 1989): 119-54.

        The author uses the technique of photo-interview to study
a rural Iowa farm community and shows several benefits of this
approach.   She offers a strong argument in favour of using
photography in qualitative research. Photography gives a number
of messages about reality that viewers can construct for themselves.
(See 97).

108.   Stanley, Liz. "Essays on Women's Work and Leisure and
        'Hidden' Work." Studies in Sexual Politics 18 (1987):
        1-61.

        Stresses the useful role of historical data sources in
exploring women's work and leisure. Three such inter-related data
are examined: diaries and autobiographies; the Mass Observation
Archive at the University of Sussex (England); and oral history
projects in various countries.   Emphasizes a historical
understanding of women's leisure and its relationship to work and
other aspects of life. *(See 83, 96).*

109.   Stanley, Liz (ed.). Feminist Praxis: Research, Theory and
        Epistemology in Feminist Sociology. London: Routledge,
        1990.

        The authors in this collection provide a detailed account of
feminist research and shows how feminist epistemology can be
translated into concrete research practices. This book makes an
invaluable guide for feminists carrying out research at all levels
and across many disciplines. *(See 83, 99)*.

110.   Statham, Anne; Eleanor M. Miller, and Hans O.Mauksch
        (eds.). The Worth of Women's Work: A Qualitative
        Synthesis. New York: State University of New York
        Press, 1988.

        This book challenges many common assumptions about
women's work. It integrates findings from qualitative studies of
women's experiences in 13 occupations and shows that women
devise ingenious methods for maintaining dignity in the face of
gender oppression. *(See 82, 83)*.

111.   Stone, Linda, and J. Gabriel Campbell. "The Use and
        Misuse of Surveys in International Development: An
        Experiment from Nepal." Human Organization 43, no. 1
        (Spring 1984): 27-37.

        Western survey research methods are heavily used by
developing countries. This study selects three villages in Nepal
with which researchers are familiar to show the shortcomings of a
popular KAP (knowledge, attitude, practice) survey. It emphasizes
the need for combining qualitative anthropological methods with
surveys and draws attention to the problems of survey research in
non-Western contexts. *(See 83)*.

112.   Van Maanen, John. Tales of the Field: On Writing
        Ethnography. Chicago: University of Chicago Press, 1988.

        The author discusses convention in ethnographic narrative
and the inter-relationship between doing ethnographic field work

and writing about it. *(See 86, 91)*.

1.4 Gender At Work: Women in the Labour Market

113.   Abraham, M. Francis, and P. Subhadra Abraham (eds).
        Women, Development and Change: The Third World
        Experience. Bristol, IN: Wyndham, 1988.

A collection of recent scholarship by 15 researchers in the
field of women's studies and the Third World. The contributions
fall under two categories: theoretical analysis of various
perspectives on gender inequity; and empirical study of women's
participation in the economy, particularly in the informal sector.
(See 28, 161, 312).

114.   Afshar, Haleh. Work and Ideology in the Third World.
        New York: Tavistock Publications, 1985.

This book explores the sources and consequences of
discrimination against women in the labour market. It addresses
the invisibility of women's work and argues that cultural, political
and ideological factors play a central role in determining women's
position. It documents the way in which traditional values affect
women's lives in developing countries, even as societies undergo
rapid change. *(See 2, 136)*.

115.   Allan, S., and C. Wolkowitz. Home-working: Myths and
        Realities. London: Macmillan, 1987.

The authors demonstrate the growing importance of home-
working for the capitalist mode of production and question the
conventional assumptions about home-working. It is argued that
home workers are cheap and flexible, and therefore profitable for
the capitalist system. *(See 117, 119, 304)*.

116.   Anker, Richard, and Catherine Hein (eds.).   Sex
        Inequalities in Urban Employment in the Third World.
        London: Macmillan, 1986.

This book discusses both gender inequality in the labour market and assumptions about women's lesser commitment to labour force participation. It looks at women's actual work histories and shows their high level of participation in the informal sector of the economy. *(See 2, 113)*.

117.   Benton, Lauren A.   "Homework and Industrial Development: Gender Roles and Restructuring in the Spanish Shoe Industry." World Development 17, no. 2 (February 1989): 255-66.

Analyses the changing role of homework in the Spanish shoe industry. Traces the patterns of mobility between factory work and homework in an export-oriented industry and examines the effects of the restructuring of capital on homework. Concludes that the sub-standard working conditions endured by homeworkers have a negative impact on women and on industrial development. *(See 115, 119)*.

118.   Blau, Francine D., and Marianne A. Ferber. The Economics of Women, Men and Work. New Jersey: Prentice Hall, 1986.

This book focuses on 'economic woman' and is a text that acquaints students with the findings of recent research on women, men and work in the labour market and in the household. *(See 113, 125, 162)*.

119.   Boris, Eileen, and Cynthia R. Daniels (eds.). Homework: Historical and Contemporary Perspectives on Paid Labor at Home. Urbana: University of Illinois Press, 1989.

This research uses case studies and offers a rich historical picture of home-based labour. It stresses the importance of class, race and gender in comprehending the history of homework. The authors raise a concern that the recent trend in the growth of homework could herald the return of the 'sweatshop.' *(See 115, 117)*.

120.   Chaplin, David. "Domestic Service and Industrialization."
        Comparative Studies in Sociology 1 (1978): 97-127.

        Uses various theoretical perspectives to provide a
comparative study of the neglected topic of domestic service.
Domestic service is seen as a prime social indicator of the level of
industrialization of a country.

121.   Committee for Asian Women.   International Women
        Workers. Special issue of ISIS International, September,
        no. 4, 1985.

        This issue focuses on working women in export oriented
industries and in the newly industrialized countries in Asia. It
demonstrates the common problems shared by working women and
provides stark examples of assault on working women as well as
women's resistance to oppressive working conditions. (See 132).

122.   D'Amico Samuels, Deborah. You Can't Get Me Out of
        the Race: Women and Economic Development in Negril,
        Jamaica, West Indies. Ph.D. Dissertation in Anthropology.
        New York: The City University of New York, 1986.

        This study brings theories of discrimination into the centre
of the economics of women's labour in order to improve our
conceptualization of women's labour and to enhance our
formulation of labour in general. It illuminates some previously
ignored corners of the modern labour market. (See 128).

123.   DeVault, Marjorie L. Women and Food: Housework and
        the Production of Family Life. Ph.D. Dissertation,
        Northwestern University, Evanston Illinois, 1984.

        This Ph.D. thesis discusses unrecognized aspects of
housework in contemporary urban households. The study is based
on interviews conducted in thirty households in metropolitan
Chicago during 1982-83. (See 129).

124.   Delphy, Christine. Close to Home: A Materialist Analysis

of Women's Oppression. Amherst: The University of
Massachusetts Press, 1984.

By focusing on housework, the author raises central
questions in the study of women. She is critical of Marxist
methodology regarding women's domestic work and sees
patriarchal ideology in the family as playing a central role in the
subordination of women. This book provides a strategy for
women's liberation. *(See 123, 133)*.

125. Game, Ann, and Rosemary Pringle. Gender At Work.
      London: Pluto Press, 1984.

This book provides a comparative approach in studying
gender identities on the job. It discusses the nature of gender
construction and how different aspects of work have gender-
specific labels. It also argues that the automation of the labour
process may challenge male domination. *(See 118)*.

126. Harcourt, Wendy. "Gender, Culture, and Reproduction:
      North and South." Development (SID) 2-3 (1988): 66-71.

Examines the culturally and historically specific
development of gynaecology and obstetric medicine in North
America. The author draws attention to the negative and positive
effects of this development and shows that we can have some say
about the influence of medicine on our bodies. In a parallel
fashion, the author argues that female circumcision in Africa
should be questioned. *(See 114, 381, 483)*.

127. Kramer, Laura (ed.). Sociology of Gender: A Text
      Reader. Scarborough: Nelson of Canada, 1991.

The collection of articles in this text provides a rich
perspective on the complex dimensions of gender relations. It
shows that gender is reproduced through a complex interaction of
economics, politics, and culture. *(See 53, 55)*.

128. Leacock, Eleanor; Helen I. Safa and Contributors.

Women's Work: Development and Division of Labour by
Gender. Mass.: Bergin and Garvey Publishers Inc., 1986.

The author looks at gender inequality both at home and in
the wider society, and questions the separation between public and
private lives. Women's productive and reproductive roles are
intertwined and a strategy for change has to address both of these
levels. *(See 122).*

129.   Long, Norman (ed.). Family and Work in Rural Societies:
        Perspectives on Non-Wage-Labour. London: Tavistock
        Publications, 1984.

The contributors to this book examine the character and
significance of unpaid household agricultural and domestic work
and inter-household or community-level labour exchanges. They
look at the changing nature of women's work and the importance
of non-paid labour for the survival of both the family and
community. *(See 123).*

130.   Loutfi, Martha F. Rural Women: Unequal Partners in
        Development. Geneva: ILO, 1985.

This monograph draws together the principal themes that
arise regarding rural women's work. It places official policies in
perspective and provides new directions. It also brings out some
general realities concerning women in all societies and demands the
equal partnership of women in development projects. *(See 135,
284, 343,* 348).

131.   Nuss, Shirley (in collaboration with Ettore Denti and David
        Viry). Women in the World of Work: Statistical Analysis
        and Projections to the Year 2000. Geneva: ILO, 1989.

This book provides statistical information and an analysis
of male and female economic activity at global, regional and
national levels. It evaluates past trends and future prospects by
age, economic sector and years of working life. *(See 125).*

132.   Peña, Devon, and Gilbert Cardenas. "The Division of
       Labor in Microelectronics: A Comparative Analysis of
       France, Mexico, and the United States."   Studies in
       Comparative International Development 23, no. 2 (Summer
       1988): 89-112.

       Focuses on the microelectronic industry and provides a
comparative analysis of the shop floor division of labour. The
three case studies reveal a universal gender-based division of
labour. *(See 121)*.

133.   Redclift, Manneke, and Enzo Mingione (eds.).   Beyond
       Employment: Household, Gender and Subsistence. Oxford:
       Basil Blackwell, 1985.

       This book examines the complex relationships between
family and the household and the wider economy. It is informed
by recent theoretical debates, uses examples from around the world
and shows the link between formal and informal sectors of the
economy.   The contributors discuss the social relations of
production with an emphasis on women's work. *(See 124, 134)*.

134.   Reeves, Joy B. "Work and Family Roles: Contemporary
       Women in Indonesia." Sociological Spectrum 7, no. 3
       (1986): 223-42.

       Looks at family-work integration and compares the U.S.
with Indonesia. Concludes that there is less sex-based stratification
in Indonesia than in the U.S. Women can also achieve family-
work integration relatively easier than in the U.S. As Indonesia
develops economically, it is predicted that we will see the growth
of sex-based stratification. *(See 124, 133)*.

135.   Rossini, Rosa Ester.   "Women as Labor Force in
       Agriculture: The Case of the State of St. Paulo, Brazil."
       Studi-Emigrazione 20, 70 (June 1983): 222-230.

       Provides a general discussion of women's work and the
problems of working women. This case study criticizes the census

definition of economically active, discusses women's double work-day and their subordinate position in the labour market. *(See 130)*.

136.   Taplin, Ruth. "Women and Work in Egypt: A Social Historical Perspective." International Sociology 2, no. 1 (March 1987): 61-76.

Questions theories of women's work in the Muslim Arab world. Provides historical evidence from Egypt to show that Muslim women have always participated in the labour force, both on an informal and formal basis. This paper discusses various types of work done by different classes of women in the five stages of Egypt's economic development. *(See 114)*.

137.   Ward, Kathryn (ed.).   Women Workers and Global Restructuring. Cornell University: ILR Press, 1990.

This collection uses multiple methodology to look at the impact of the changes that the global economy has had on the lives of Third World working women. It illuminates multiple roles of women, both in the formal and informal sectors of the economy, and their ties with the global economic system. *(See 7, 12, 19, 372)*.

1.5 Working for Change

138.   Adamson, Nancy, Linda Briskin, and Margaret McPhail. Feminist Organizing for Change: The Contemporary Women's Movement in Canada.   Toronto: Oxford University Press, 1988.

Documents and analyses the struggle of the contemporary women's movement in introducing change. It makes a distinction between grassroots and institutionalized feminism, and by emphasizing the former, reveals a part of feminist organizing that has often been invisible.

139.   Albrecht, Lisa, and Rose M. Brewer (eds.). Bridges of

Power: Women's Multicultural Alliances. Philadelphia: New Society Publishers, 1990.

This book presents the voices of women of colour, poor women, working-class women and women from the countries of the South, community-based women and all the women who have transformed the face of feminism. It provides us with success stories of women's alliances. *(See 170).*

140. Aptheker, Bettina. Tapestries of Life: Women's Work, Women's Consciousness, and the Meaning of Daily Experience. Amherst: The University of Massachussets Press, 1989.

This book explores women's ways of seeing through the use of stories, life histories, poems and printings by women from different races, ages, social classes, and sexual preferences. While the focus is on the United States, the findings and methodology are useful for other situations. *(See 87, 88, 105).*

141. Burkey, Stan. People First: A Guide to Self-Reliant Participatory Rural Development. London: Zed Books, 1993.

Based on grassroots, popularly controlled, environmentally friendly development activity, the author provides a methodology for achieving local development. An important source for those involved in development issues. *(See 29, 76, 148, 351).*

142. Colburn, Forrest D. (ed.). Everyday Forms of Peasant Resistance. Princeton: Princeton University Press, 1990.

This collection enhances our understanding of popular resistance against authorities who are perceived to be unjust. It provides a new insight into rural social relations and is rich both theoretically and ethnographically. *(See 138, 182).*

143. Davies, Miranda. Third World Second Sex: Women's Struggles and National Liberation; Third World Women

Speak Out. London: Zed Books, 1983.

This book is a compilation of interviews and articles by women from the Third World. They belong to women from countries as diverse as Oman, Bolivia, India, Mauritius and Zimbabwe. The publication reveals how Third World women are confronting traditional male dominated structures with courage, and provides a useful list of women's organizations. *(See 44)*.

144.   Fennelly Levy, Marion. Each in Her Own Way: Five Women Leaders of the Developing World. Boulder: Lynne Rienner Publishers, 1988.

This collection of biographies of five women describes some of the social and economic changes that are affecting the developing world-changes that often have negative impacts on the lives of poor women. The five women interviewed in this book, each in her own way, tried to bring about positive changes. *(See 74, 149, 567)*.

145.   Garland, Anne Witte. Women Activists Challenge the Abuse of Power. New York: The Feminist Press at the City University of New York, 1988.

This book gives voice to ordinary women, including blue collar and middle class, and their concerns about everyday life issues. It addresses central issues of women's concerns and shows how ordinary women can affect social change. This book shows how one person can make a difference. *(See 74, 144, 150)*.

146.   Hooks, Bell. Sisters of the Yam: Black Women and Self-Recovery. Toronto: Between the Lines, 1993.

This self-help book successfully develops links between our individual efforts to be self-actualized and collective liberation struggles. The author touches on diverse issues and provides strategies to empower women to struggle against racism and patriarchy. *(See 42, 74, 143)*.

147.   Jayawardena, Kumari.   Feminism and Nationalism in the
       Third World.   London: Zed Books, 1986.

       The author gives detailed accounts of women's movements
in a number of countries- India, Sri Lanka, China, Indonesia,
Vietnam, Japan, Korea, and the Philippines. This book challenges
the view that feminism is a foreign ideology currently being
imposed on the Third World countries. *(See 143, 161, 379, 650)*.

148.   Max-Neef, Manfred.   From the Outside Looking in:
       Experiences in 'Barefoot Economics'. London: Zed Books,
       1992.

       This publication provides a critical analysis of orthodox
development economics and presents a fresh approach to meeting
human needs through the self-reliant activities of a grassroots
population.   It demonstrates the importance of the active
participation of people in improving their lives. *(See 76, 141)*.

149.   Seabrook, Jeremy.   Pioneers of Change: Experiments in
       Creating a Humane Society. London: Zed Books, 1993.

       An account of some remarkable individuals and movements
from developed and developing countries who are experimenting
with new paths of development and new relations with nature. It
offers a challenge to the Western view of development. *(See 144,
354)*.

150.   Wignarajan, Ponna (ed.).   New Social Movements in the
       South.   London: Zed Books, 1992.

       This edition brings forward the views of some of the most
outstanding intellectuals in the Third World. These intellectuals
attempt to transform the lives of the poor and also work to
establish political and economic democracy in the Third World.
The author discusses the diversity of the new social movement for
change in the South. *(See 144, 145, 362)*.

Chapter Two

Africa

2.1 Women of Africa: An Introduction

151. Bullwinkle, Davis A. African Women: A General Bibliography, 1976-1985. New York: Greenwood Press, 1989.

   This bibliography provides a long list of sources on African women regarding all aspects of their lives, from economic, to politics, to culture. The author has also a similar compilation on women in various countries in Africa. *(See 152)*.

152. Coles, Catherine M., and Barbara Entwiste. Nigerian Women in Development: A Research Bibliography. University of California, Crossroads Press, 1985.

   This bibliography focuses on women's role in the economy and provides a long list of items on various aspects of women's lives in Nigeria. *(See 151)*.

153. Croll, Elizabeth J. "Women in Rural Production and Reproduction in the Soviet Union, China, Cuba, and Tanzania: Case Studies." Signs 7, no. 2 (Winter 1981): 375-99.

   Looks at women's experiences with development programs in four socialist countries: Soviet Union, China, Cuba, and

Tanzania. Shows that in these programs, women's reproductive and domestic roles were not redefined. The result has been an intensification of women's labour. Although this article shows the achievements of socialist countries, it reveals the existence of inequalities, the sexual division of labour and the absence of well-defined policies concerning reproductive spheres. *(See 333, 348, 432)*.

154.   Cutrufelli, Maria Rosa. <u>Women of Africa: Roots of Oppression</u>. London: Zed Press, 1983.

The author attempts to increase our knowledge of African Women's position by means of this book. She shows the complexity of women's position, as well as their fast changing world. *(See 156, 580, 583, 598, 599)*.

155.   Guyer, Jane I., and other commentators. "The Multiplication of Labour: Historical Methods in the Study of Gender and Agricultural Change in Modern Africa." <u>Current Anthropology</u> 29, no. 2 (April 1988): 247-59 (259-72 include comments and reply).

Emphasizes the value of longitudinal data in studying the division of labour in Africa and the difficulty of getting comparable data for different periods. Suggests an alternative approach, an analysis based on the concepts of "habitus," "rhythms," and "key tasks" in explaining the division of labour. Uses this approach to analyze social change among the Beti and shows how new cropping patterns, cash incomes, and conflicts between men and women are articulated by farming cycles. *(See 85, 92)*.

156.   Hay, Margaret Jean, and Sharon Stichter (eds.). <u>African Women: South of the Sahara</u>. London: Longman, 1984.

Using a multi-disciplinary approach, the authors provide a comprehensive survey of the economic, social and political roles of women in Africa, both in the past and present. *(See 154, 158)*.

157.   House, William J. "The Status of Women in the Sudan."

Journal of Modern African Studies 26, no. 2 (June 1988): 277-302.

Discusses women's position in Sudan. Although women are active in economic life, especially in agriculture, official statistics underestimate their roles. Women are discriminated against socially and culturally, and as a result they have a subordinate position in all levels of public life. *(See 154).*

158. Ivan-Smith, Edda, Nidhi Tandon and Jane Connors. Women in Sub-Saharan Africa. London: The Minority Rights Group, Report #77, 1988.

Three authors with experience in the region provide a survey of women's life in Sub-Saharan Africa. All three discuss the particular problems of women living in South Africa and in countries which are economically tied to it. *(See 156).*

159. Milimo, Mabel C. "Women, Population and Food in Africa: The Zambian Case." Development: Seeds of Change 2-3 (1987): 70-83.

Focuses on the rapid increase of the population and the crisis of food production in Zambia. Analyses the historical root of the problem and argues that the patriarchal system, a legacy of colonialism, has denied women access to productive resources. Suggests strategies for addressing the problems in order to enable women to increase their production of food. *(See 13, 16, 396, 596).*

160. Nelson, Nici. (ed.). African Women in the Development Process. London: Frank Cass and Company Ltd., 1981.

With the exception of one paper, all articles concentrate on sub-Saharan Africa. They mainly deal with specific situations in which African women find themselves, ranging widely from sub-elite nurses in Zambia to the efforts of uneducated women in Nigeria to form a cooperative. The contributors explore a number of common themes in women's lives and provide a profile of women in different socio-economic contexts. *(See 2, 158, 197, 604).*

161.   Presley, Cora Ann.   "The Mau Mau Rebellion, Kikuyu
       Women, and Social Change." Revue canadienne des études
       africaines/Canadian Journal of African Studies 22, no. 3
       (1988): 502-527.

       The research shows that women have played a central role
in Kenyan nationalism and in Mau Mau.   The development of
nationalist sentiment and activity among women has been ignored
by researchers, and the result has been an inaccurate presentation
of Kenyan nationalism.   Viewing Mau Mau from a women's
perspective adds to our understanding of the rebellion. *(See 113, 147).*

162.   Robertson, Claire.   "Invisible Workers: African Women
       and the Problem of the Self-Employed in Labour History."
       Journal of Asian and African Studies 23, nos. 1-2 (Jan-
       April 1988): 180-98.

       Calls for new frontiers of research in African labour history
and concentrates on the place of women.   Reconceptualizes the role
of women in general, their work in the urban informal sector, and
their agricultural labour.   Uses feminist analysis to question
traditional categories. *(See 118, 169).*

163.   Schoepf, Brooke Grundfest, and Claude Schoepf.   "Food
       Crisis and Agrarian Change in the Eastern Highlands of
       Zaire." Urban Anthropology 16, no. 1 (Spring 1987): 5-37.

       Presents a dynamic view of struggles over resources in one
area of Zaire.   Shows that the food crisis has deep roots and is
related to patterns of landholding, political power, and gender
roles.   The crisis is being exacerbated by accumulation strategies
pursued by the dominant classes that continue to exploit peasant
producers.   The issues related both to peasant producers and
women as the major food producers are fundamental to the food
crisis. *(See 16, 159, 596).*

164.   Simard, Gisele. "La recherche sociale dans des sociétés de paroles ou Le défi de la recherche sociale en Afrique: le cas du Cameroon." Sociologie et Sociétés 20, no. 1 (April 1988): 83-96.

This case study presents a solution to analytical problems in social research in developing countries. The focus group method, an oral methodology, proved most useful in studying African families. *(See 84, 87, 105).*

2.2 The Social Construction of Gender

165.   Callaway, Barbara, and Lucy Creevey. The Heritage of Islam: Women, Religion, and Politics in West Africa. Boulder: Lynne Rienner Publishers, 1993.

The authors explore the impact of Islam on women's lives. They address women's role in the economy, both with regard to wage-labour and the informal sector, politics and education. They provide a rich comparison between Muslim women's experiences and those of Western women. *(See 113, 136, 261).*

166.   Ensminger, Jean. "Economic and Political Differentiation among Galoloe Orma Women." Ethnos 52, nos. 1-2 (1987): 28-49.

Analyses the formal and informal power of women among cattle-raising households and measures the impact of sedentarization and cash-crop production on women's power position.

167.   Lambek, Michael. "Virgin Marriage and the Autonomy of Women in Mayotte." Signs 9, no. 2 (Winter 1983): 264-81.

Aims to understand the place of virgin marriage in the social construction of women in Mayotte, an island in the Comoro Archipelago of the West Indian Ocean. Looks at wedding rituals to show the complexity of the process that transforms a child into an adult woman and the significant role of the virgin bride in this process. Through this study the author questions how women are victims of their sexuality. *(See 187)*.

168.   Pankhurst, Helen. Gender, Development and Identity: an Ethiopian Study. London: Zed Books, 1993.

This study looks at the inter-relationship between the state, economy, religion and family in Ethiopia.   It examines the peasants' response to state policies and intervention.   This is a rich ethnography of rural women's day-to-day lives. *(See 2, 17, 604)*.

169.   Safilios-Rothschild, Constantina.   "The Persistence of Women's Invisibility in Agriculture: Theoretical and Policy Lessons from Lesotho and Sierra Leone." Economic Development and Cultural Change 33, no. 2 (January 1985): 299-317.

Uses two cases from sub-Saharan Africa to argue that a sex-based stratification system permeates norms, values, and social structures, creating mechanisms that hide rural women's contribution to agriculture in Third World countries.   Provides examples of institutional mechanisms that help keep women's work and income contributions invisible. *(See 162)*.

170.   Smith, Sheila.   "Zimbabwean Women in Co-operatives: Participation and Sexual Equality in Four Producer Co-Operatives." Journal of Social Development in Africa 2, no. 1 (1987): 29-47.

Discusses the issue of sexual equality in socialist countries. This case study suggests that in Zimbabwe, women made more progress than in other socialist countries.   However, women are responsible for most of the work.   Identifies factors which hinder women's full participation and provides recommendations. *(See 123, 139)*.

171.   Talle,   Aud.   "Women   as   Heads   of   Houses: The

Organization of Production and the Role of Women among Pastoral Maasai in Kenya." Ethnos 52, nos. 1-2 (1987): 50-80.

Discusses the power of women in a pastoral society in Kenya. Women are relatively autonomous in the household, but commercialization is decreasing women's power. *(See 130, 185)*.

172.   Thiam, Awa. Black Sisters, Speak Out: Feminism and Oppression in Black Africa. London: Pluto Press, 1986.

The author focuses on the concept of power and argues that polygamy, clitoridectomy, and sewing up the vagina are the weapon used by men to control women in Africa. The author argues that these practices are not remote, but part of a pattern of universal violence from men towards women. This book calls for direct political action which is linked to international feminism. *(See 43, 44, 583)*.

2.3 Women, State and Development Policies

173.   Aidoo, Agnes Akosua. "Women and Food Security: The Opportunity for Africa." Development (SID) 2-3 (1988): 56-62.

For the last two decades, Africa has been facing a food crisis. Among the critical factors which account for this crisis, the author analyses the blindness of development programs towards women's contributions to the production of food in Africa. Women play a major role in agriculture and the development of food, and offer Africa an opportunity to reorganize its food production programs to ensure self-reliant development. *(See 159, 163, 596)*.

174.   Borger-Poulsen, Kirsten. "Integration or Segregation?-The Gap Between Good Intentions and Appropriate Actions in Africa." Community Development Journal 20, no. 3 (July 1985) 176-83.

Women in Africa are overburdened with work and do not have much chance to take part in decision making. This paper argues that the integration of women into the development process is not just a matter of benevolent attitudes, but a requirement for development. *(See 17, 173).*

175.   Bryson, Judy C. "Women and Agriculture in Sub-Saharan Africa: Implications for Development (An Exploratory Study)." Journal of Development Studies 17, no. 3 (April 1981): 29-46.

Despite the well-documented fact that women are central to the production of food in Africa, agricultural and development economists still fail to consider which policies would build most effectively on the existing division of labour in food crop production. This study argues that the failure to recognize women's contribution in food production has contributed to the current food crisis. *(See 2, 27, 159, 593).*

176.   Caplan, Pat. "Development Policies in Tanzania--Some Implications for Women." Journal of Development Studies 17, no. 3 (April 1981): 98-108.

This field-work research on Tanzania shows that under the traditional system women enjoyed a large degree of autonomy. It supports the recent development planning policies, but calls for a policy that ensures the autonomy of individuals, rather than their dependence. This means, among other things, constructing a society where patriarchy, ageism, and sexism have no place. *(See 3, 17, 78, 578, 587).*

177.   Carr, Marilyn, and Ruby Sandhu. Women, Technology and Rural Productivity: An Analysis of the Impact of Time and Energy Saving Technologies on Women. Occasional Paper no. 6 New York: UNIFEM, 1987.

This study was funded by the United Nations Development Fund for Women (UNIFEM). It attempts to measure the extent to which technology benefits rural women. Factors which affect

women's access to technology and allow them to have more time
are complex. *(See 3).*

178.   Hansen, Karen Tranberg. "The Urban Informal Sector as
        a Development Issue: Poor Women and Work in Lusaka,
        Zambia." Urban Anthropology 9, no. 2 (Summer 1980):
        199-225.

        The increasing poverty of the Third World has become a
concern for governments and international development agencies.
The informal sector has been regarded as an opportunity for
generating employment. This paper uses the case of Lusaka,
Zambia, to criticize this approach to development. Such an
approach not only does not address the problem, but also works
particularly against the interest of poor women. *(See 8, 12, 24,
200, 296, 391, 568).*

179.   Kuzwayo, Ellen. Sit Down and Listen: Stories from South
        Africa. London: The Women's Press, 1990.

        A collection of stories that explore the complex life of the
contemporary black South Africa. They bring out the
consequences of racism and the State apparatus that enforces it.
(See 34, 88, 90).

180.   Marshall, Susan E. "Politics and Female Status in North
        Africa: A Reconsideration of Development Theory."
        Economic Development and Cultural Change 32, no. 3
        (April 1984): 499-524.

        This paper criticizes two theories of development for their
inability to explain the variations in women's status in five North
African countries. It provides a theoretical framework to explain
divergent patterns of female participation and highlights the role of
elites and government policies in promoting women's access to
modern sectors.

181.   Mbilinyi, Marjorie. "Agribusiness and Women Peasants in
        Tanzania." Development and Change 19, no. 4 (October

1988): 549-83.

This article looks at the development of agriculture in
Tanzania.   Independent commodity production increasingly
disintegrated and gave way to large-scale capitalist production.
The latter was supported by World Bank policies. In this process
women, who were involved in small-scale production, were forced
to become casual wage-workers. *(See 16)*.

182.   Nelson, Nici.   "Mobilizing Village Women: Some
        Organisational and Management Considerations." Journal
        of Development Studies 17, no. 3 (April 1981): 47-58.

Argues that if development is to take place, women should
have a meaningful participation in its programs. Discusses some
of the considerations important to programs which aim to involve
women in development. Emphasizes the significance of recruiting
female staff and management and the need for local consultation.
(See 142).

183.   Okeyo, Achola-Pala.   "The Role of Women in Eastern
        African Rural Development."   Regional Development
        Dialogue 9, no. 2 (Summer 1988): 89-101.

Policy formulation and development programs have not yet
recognized and incorporated the centrality of women's roles in
Third World countries.   This paper provides evidence to this
effect, and shows why gender-based inequality persists and what is
needed to empower women. *(See 2, 28, 153, 160, 593)*.

184.   Parpart, Jane L., and Kathleen A. Staudt. (eds.). Women
        and the State in Africa. Boulder: Lynne Rienner Publishers,
        1988.

The introductory chapter of this study provides a
comprehensive overview of theories of state, and is followed by
rich ethnographic studies which document the impact of state
policies on women. This study demonstrates the centrality of
gender in understanding state policies. *(See 27)*.

2.4 Work and Family

185.   Baroin, Catherine.   "The Position of Tubu Women in
        Pastoral Production: Daza Kesherda, Republic of Niger."
        Ethnos 52, nos. 1-2 (1987): 137-55.

Discusses the position of Tubu women in pastoral
production and shows that women's right to livestock is
fundamental for understanding their position in society. *(See 171,
342)*.

186.   Greenstreet, Miranda.   "Education and Reproductive
        Choices in Ghana: Gender Issues in Population Policy."
        Development (SID) 1 (1990): 40-47.

Argues that family planning is an essential component of
development programs. Most family planning focuses on women
and ignores the central role that men play in decisions related to
family size. Discusses social factors which contribute to high
fertility and provides recommendations to promote a better
population policy. *(See 13)*.

187.   Isiugo-Abanihe, Uche C.   "Child Fosterage in West
        Africa." Population and Development Review 11, no. 1
        (March 1985): 53-73.

Provides much evidence of child fosterage in West Africa.
Children are transferred from natal or biological homes to other
homes where they are raised and cared for by foster parents. This
paper explains the various types of child fosterage and explores its
demographic implications. This study questions the Western notion
of universal "mothering" and "parenting." *(See 76, 167)*.

188.   Jones, Jacqueline. Labor of Love, Labor of Sorrow: Black
        Women, Work, and Family from Slavery to the Present.
        New York: Basic books, 1985.

The author compares black women's work with that of
white women and discusses the impact of their work on their

families, communities and their personal relationships. She shows that black women's history of wage labour is that of agricultural work, domestic labour and industrial work, all of which are mainly cheap labour. *(See 42, 46)*.

189.   Kenyon, Susan, M. <u>Five Women of Sennar: Culture and Change in Central Sudan</u>. Oxford: Clarendon Press, 1991.

The crisis of recent years has brought far-reaching changes in Sudan. The author looks at some of these changes and opportunities through the eyes and words of five women from the town of Sennar, Blue Nile Province. In this book, women talk about their families and homes, their hopes and aspirations, their work and their social lives. These accounts offer an insight into life in a contemporary Sudanese town, from the perspective of both ordinary and extraordinary women. *(See 90, 584)*.

190.   Little, Peter D. "Woman as Ol Payian (Elder): The Status of Widows among the Il Chamus (Njemps) of Kenya." <u>Ethnos</u> 52, nos. 1-2 (1987): 81-102.

The author argues that the type of work women are expected to do and can do is dependent on their position at a particular stage of the life cycle. However, widowhood changes the pattern of behaviour and opens new opportunities for women.

191.   Okpala, Amon O. "Female Employment and Family among Urban Nigerian Women." <u>Journal of Developing Areas</u> 23, no. 3 (April 1989): 439-56.

Examines the relationship between labour force participation and fertility. Discusses variations in fertility by the types of occupation that women hold. Offers data on women's labour force participation and makes some suggestions for future policy and research. *(See 152)*.

192.   Omari, C. K.   "Politics and Policies of Food Self-Sufficiency in Tanzania." <u>Social Science and Medicine</u> 22, no. 7 (1986): 769-774.

Discusses the government's attempts and policies to improve food production and distribution in order to upgrade the nutritional status in the country. Criticizes the programs for their overemphasis on political development and argues that in the case of food crop production and nutrition the success will depend on the extent to which labour force at the household level is utilized. *(See 159, 163, 173)*.

193. Schuster, Ilsa. "Kinship, Life Cycle, and Education in Lusaka." Journal of Comparative Family Studies 18, no. 3 (Autumn 1987): 363-387.

Argues that kin relations remain deeply important in Zambian society. Most Zambians have blood relatives for security. The importance of blood is reinforced by the transience of the marital bond and the absence of State welfare. *(See 190, 191)*.

194. Suda, Collette. "Differential Participation of Men and Women in Production and Reproduction in Kakamega District." Journal of Developing Societies 5, no. 2 (July-Oct 1989): 234-44.

Women play a central role in agricultural production in Kenya. This paper discusses the gender division of labour on family farms. It shows that changes in the traditional structure of the division of labour have created extra responsibilities for women. Women are overworked and underpaid. Calls for government policies to diminish women's workload. *(See 2, 159, 163)*.

195. Vaughan, Megan, and Henrietta Moore. "Health, Nutrition and Agricultural Development in Northern Zambia." Social Science and Medicine 27, no. 7 (1988): 743-45.

In order to adequately address the problem of nutrition and health in Africa, we have to look at women's position in kinship and in agricultural production. Women play a central role in food production while they are also in charge of domestic labour. This heavy burden of work can have unforeseen consequences for their health and that of their children. *(See 159, 163)*.

196.   Watts, Susan J. "Marriage Migration, a Neglected Form of Long-Term Mobility: A Case Study from Ilorin, Nigeria." International Migration Review 17, no. 4 (Winter 1983): 682-98.

This article examines the significance of marriage migration in Ilorin, Nigeria. It shows that rural women marry into wealthy polygamous urban compounds and return to their native rural compounds later in life. It concludes that women must not be regarded as pawns in a power game. *(See 10, 374)*.

2.5 Women's Experience of Wage-work

197.   Chan, Stephen. "Young Women and Development in Africa-Some Generally Unconsidered Considerations." Community Development Journa 18, no. 3 (October 1983): 257-62.

Draws attention to the major problem of youth unemployment in Africa. As a generation, youth, especially young women, have a bleak future. Young women have a disadvantaged position in the formal and informal sectors of the economy. As well, national and international agencies do not pay equal attention to the needs of young women. *(See 160)*.

198.   Cock, Jacklyn. Maids and Madams: A Study in the Politics of Exploitation. Johannesburg: Ravan Press, 1980.

This book looks at South African black women domestic workers, who comprise the largest percentage of working women in any occupational category in South Africa, and challenges the views about the relationships between 'maids' and 'madams' in white south African households. It raises challenging issues by looking at the stories told by black women themselves. *(See 34, 41, 299, 400, 433, 586, 595)*.

199.   Dennis, Carolyne. "Women in African Labour History."
       Journal of Asian and African Studies 23, nos. 1-2 (January-
       April 1988): 125-40.

Discusses the issues which have dominated different
perspectives within African labour history. Argues that labour
history in Africa has focused on men's labour because it has
concentrated on wage-labour. In order to develop a labour theory
which incorporates women's labour, we need to look outside the
boundaries of "formal" labour theory. *(See 162, 585).*

200.   Diouf, Made Bandé.   "Les restauratrices de la zone
       industrielle de Dakar, ou La guerre des marmites." Cahiers
       d'Études Africaines 21, nos. 1-3 (81-83, 1981): 237-50.

This analysis of the restaurant business shows the
relationship between the so-called formal and informal sector.
Discusses the role of the State and shows how migrant rural
women serve as cheap labour in the restaurants in the cities. *(See
178, 391).*

201.   Dorsey, Betty Jo. "Academic Women at the University of
       Zimbabwe: Career Prospects, Aspirations and Family Role
       Constraints." Zimbabwe Journal of Educational Research
       1, no. 3 (November 1989): 342-76.

Provides general information on women academics in
Zimbabwe and examines factors that affect academic career
prospects for women.   Family responsibilities and social
expectations negatively affect women's position in the University.
Concludes that a patriarchal society, such as Zimbabwe, enhances
the position of men and relegates women to a subordinate position.
(See 191).

202.   Edwards, Nancy C. "Traditional Mende Society in Sierra
       Leone: A Sociocultural Basis for a Quantitative Research
       Study." Health Care for Women International 10, no. 1
       (Winter 1989): 1-14.

This study of Traditional Birth Attendants (TBAs) in Sierra Leone shows the important role that TBAs play in maternal child care in developing countries. It highlights a number of important questions that should be asked by researchers intending to undertake such studies. *(See 83, 92)*.

203.   Kerven, Carol. "Academics, Practitioners and All Kinds of Women in Development: A Reply to Peters." Journal of Southern African Studies 10, no. 2 (April 1984): 259-268.

A response to Pauline Peters' article on development cycles and women in Botswana. Argues that Peters presents a biased account of female farmers in Botswana. *(See 206)*.

204.   Lawson, Lesley. Working Women in South Africa. London: Pluto Press, 1986.

Addresses various aspects of women's lives in South Africa. Provides much information on women's work in the factories, in the rural areas, in the formal and informal sectors, and in the household. Shows that women's struggle and their organizations have played a major part in improving their lives. *(See 158, 198, 585)*.

205.   Okojie, Christiana E. "Female Migrants in the Urban Labour Market: Benin City, Nigeria." Revue canadienne des etudes africaines 18, no. 3 (1984): 547-62.

The labour force participation of migrant women resembles that of non-migrants. Education is the determining factor for opening doors for women's employment. *(See 10, 196, 585)*.

206.   Peters, Pauline. "Gender, Developmental Cycles and Historical Process: A Critique of Recent Research on Women in Botswana." Journal of Southern African Studies 10, no. 1 (October 1983): 100-22.

This article illustrates the shortcomings of an undifferentiated perspective in understanding migrant labour in

Southern Africa. It focuses on Botswana and Lesotho, points to empirical gaps and suggests directions for future research. *(See 203)*.

207.   Schildkrout, Enid.   "Children's Work Reconsidered." International Social Science Journal 32, no. 3 (1980): 479-89.

Looks at conceptual issues important in defining and understanding the nature of children's work. Child labour in the informal sector is discussed and related to female employment in northern Nigeria. *(See 8, 197)*.

208.   Swantz, Marja-Lisa.   "The Identity of Women in African Development." Development: Seeds of Change 2-3 (1987): 19-24.

Argues that the invisibility of women's work contributes to the decline of national development programs. Women's invisibility is not simply a matter of women's welfare, but has detrimental economic, social, and political consequences at national and international levels. Concludes that a balanced development program must have women's input. *(See 160)*.

209.   Tinker, Irene.   "Street Foods: Testing Assumptions about Informal Sector Activity by Women and Men." Current Sociology 35, no. 3 (Winter 1987): i-110.

This issue focuses on street vending to show the importance of the informal sector in generating income in developing countries. Data from the Philippines, Indonesia, Bangladesh, Senegal, Nigeria, and Egypt show that women play an important part in this sector, but remain invisible. The street food project calls on the government to recognize and support street food sellers and underscores the necessity of dividing data by sex. *(See 178, 200, 585)*.

2.6 Working in the Rural Areas

210.   Adams, Jennifer M.   "Female Wage Labor in Rural
        Zimbabwe." World Development 19, nos. 2-3 (February-
        March 1991): 163-77.

This article emphasizes rural women's role as wage workers
and discusses the poverty that working women face in rural areas.
Shows that rural women are not homogeneous, but come from
various classes. *(See 129, 153).*

211.   Adekanye, Tomilayo O.   "Women in Agriculture in
        Nigeria: Problems and Policies for Development."
        Women's Studies International Forum 7, no. 6 (1984): 423-
        31.

Provides a short review of the place of agriculture in the
Nigerian economy. Concludes from a detailed case study, that
women are very active in various aspects of agricultural
production. Discusses the nature of women's involvement in
agriculture and suggests recommendations to improve women's
access to credit and other resources. *(See 175).*

212.   Dey, Jennie. "Gambian Women: Unequal Partners in Rice
        Development Projects?" Journal of Development Studies
        17, no. 3 (April 1981): 109-122.

This study criticizes agricultural development projects for
excluding women. While women are very active in agriculture,
their valuable expertise has gone unnoticed. By excluding women,
the projects have increased women's dependence on men. This has
not only made women more vulnerable, but has also contributed to
the deficiencies of these projects. *(See 2, 129, 130).*

213.   Gladwin, Christina H., and Della McMillan. "Is a
        Turnaround in Africa Possible Without Helping African
        Women to Farm?" Economic Development and Cultural
        Change 37, no. 2 (January 1989): 345-69.

Attempts to answer the question of whether a turnaround is
possible without giving African farmers the access to input and the

incentives they need to produce. Discusses both the positive and negative responses to this question. Recommends that policy makers, at all levels, must ensure that women are not displaced as farmers and are incorporated into the agricultural development process. *(See 113, 211).*

214.   Henn, Jeanne Koopman. "Feeding the Cities and Feeding the Peasants: What Role for Africa's Women Farmers?" World Development 11, no. 12 (December 1983): 1043-1055.

        The crisis of food in Africa could be successfully addressed by focusing on village-based food production. Women can play a central role in this process. While it is well-documented that women are Africa's primary food producers, their contribution is not acknowledged. This study uses two case studies to delineate women's problems. These problems have to be addressed if we want to solve the food crisis in Africa. *(See 130, 159, 175, 211, 596, 607).*

215.   Jiggins, Janice. "How Poor Women Earn Income in Sub-Saharan Africa and What Works Against Them." World Development 17, no. 7 (July 1989): 953-63.

        Household-based agricultural production remains the major source of food for the rural population in Sub-Saharan Africa. Women are the central core of food production, but few have opportunities to become producers and have access to services. Support for women's activities is essential if further deterioration is to be prevented. *(See 159, 175, 183).*

216.   Kachingwe, S.K. "Zimbabwe Women: A Neglected Factor in Social Development." Journal of Social Development in Africa 1, no. 1 (1986): 27-33.

        Attempts to discuss some of the major problems that women face in agricultural related activities. Although women play a central role in the production of food, they are socially, legally, and economically subordinated. Calls for the integration of women in development programs and provides recommendations. *(See 211)*.

217. Lockwood, Victoria S. <u>Tahitian Transformation: Gender and Capitalist Development in a Rural Society</u>. Boulder: Lynne Rienner Publishers, 1992.

This book shows how capitalism has penetrated the lives of rural women and has transformed their lives. This transformation has accelerated with the rapid modernization process. It provides a critical evaluation of the modernization process and its impact on women. *(See 16)*.

218. Palmer, Ingrid. "Women in Rural Development." <u>International Development Review</u> 22, nos. 2-3 (1980): 39-45.

This article is based on three case studies to show how rural development plans have ignored the interests of women. In these cases, agricultural intensification programs have increased women's workload and forced landless women to migrate to cities. This paper calls for integrating women into development programs and for paying more attention to their interests. *(See 160, 162, 607)*.

219. Staudt, Kathleen. "Uncaptured or Unmotivated? Women and the Food Crisis in Africa." <u>Rural Sociology</u> 52, no. 1 (Spring 1987): 37-55.

Addresses the food and development crisis in Africa. Uses a gendered approach to agriculture and argues that women's contribution to food production is significant. Provides policy proposals which place the needs of the majority of food producers, that is, women, first. *(See 159, 160, 596, 607)*.

220. Von Braun, Joachim, and Patrick J.R. Webb. "The Impact of New Crop Technology on the Agricultural Division of Labor in a West African Setting." <u>Economic Development and Cultural Change</u> 37, no. 3 (April 1989): 513-34.

Evaluates the impact of new technology on the division of labour in the production of rice and discusses the allocation of labour in communal and individual farming. Concludes that the transformation of production arrangements has involved more complex changes in the system than a simple change from rice being a women's crop to becoming a men's crop. *(See 3, 176).*

2.7 Working for Change

221.　Barker, Jonathan.　Rural Communities Under Stress: Peasant Farmers and the State in Africa.　Cambridge: Cambridge University Press, 1989.

The author examines forces that affect peasant communities in Sub-Sahara Africa. He draws upon a wide range of studies and shows that peasant farms have ways of defending their own interests. This book explains the limitations of the market-oriented approach to international relations and provides an alternative. *(See 22, 31).*

222.　Ladipo, Patricia. "Developing Women's Cooperatives: An Experiment in Rural Nigeria." Journal of Development Studies 17, no. 3 (April 1981): 123-36.

In the context of rural development projects, this study focuses on the experiences of two groups of Yoruba women who organized themselves along cooperative lines. It suggests that the process of cooperative formation is stressful, but helps to build skills and attitudes that women need if they are to be a part of the modernizing society. *(See 149, 354).*

223.　Mackenzie, Fiona. "Local Initiatives and National Policy: Gender and Agricultural Change in Murang'a District, Kenya." Revue canadienne des etudes africaines/Canadian Journal of African Studies 20, no. 3 (1986): 377-401.

Discusses the impact of recent agricultural policies within the context of small farms in a central province of Kenya. The national agricultural policy has fostered contradictions in the rural areas. It has enhanced polarization as well as sexual differences among the population. This study stresses the importance of women's groups in providing women with the necessary support system to face these contradictions. *(See 227).*

224.   McSweeney, Brenda Gael. "Time to Learn, Time for a Better Life: The Women's Education Project in Upper Volta." Assignment Children 49-50 (Spring 1980): 109-26.

This study of Upper Volta shows that women are overloaded with work and suffer from a low standard of living. By introducing time-saving technologies, training programs, and educational activities, women's revenue increased and they became participants in generating programs for change.

225.   Meer, Fatima (ed.). Factory and Family: The Divided Lives of South Africa's Women Workers. Durban: Institute for Black Research, 1984.

This report reveals many of the problems Black working women experience and exposes the harsh living conditions they have to endure. It is an attempt to counter sexual and racial discrimination. It is thought-provoking and shows how women, in their various capacities, try to change things. *(See 198, 204).*

226.   Okojie, Christiana. "Achieving Self-Reliance in Food Production in Nigeria: Maximizing the Contribution of Rural Women." Journal of Social Development in Africa 6, no. 2 (1991): 33-52.

Critically looks at the impact of modernization on agriculture and argues that to achieve self-reliance in food production, we must focus on women, who are the central food producers. Provides recommendations to improve women's position in society. *(See 191, 351).*

227.   Opondo, Diana. "A Women's Group in Kenya and Its Struggle to Obtain Credit." Assignment Children 49-50

(Spring 1980): 127-39.

Discusses a women's group's attempt to generate credit in order to improve their income level and their market position. This article shows the difficulties as well as the benefits of women's self-help programs and activities. *(See 223, 592, 606)*.

228.   Paul, Anne-Marie Fati.   "Women, Environment and Development: Case Studies from Ghana." Development (SID) 2-3 (1989): 84-87.

Focuses on Ghana and shows how the deteriorating environment and the problems of human settlement arising from the influx of large numbers of people into cities have affected women negatively.   Uses three case studies to demonstrate how women have participated in successful development projects. *(See 21)*.

229.   Rogers, Susan G.   "Efforts Toward Women's Development in Tanzania: Gender Rhetoric vs. Gender Realities." Women and Politics 2, no. 4 (Winter 1982): 23-41.

This paper analyses the effectiveness of the national women's organization (UWT) and other organizational efforts designed to improve the lives of poor rural women in Tanzania. It demonstrates some of the problems involved in bringing women into the development framework. *(See 2, 152, 160)*.

230.   Rondeau, Chantal.   "Paysannes du Sahel et stratégies alimentaires." Revue internationale d'action communautaire/International Review of Community Development 17(57) (Spring 1987): 63-80.

Sahel can provide an alternative model for development. In this model, the primary emphasis is on the family and community.   Resources are used to this end.   Women play a major role and challenge the patriarchal and capitalist economy. *(See 159, 236)*.

231.   Swantz, Marja-Liisa. Women in Development: A Creative
        Role Denied? The Case of Tanzania. London: C. Hurst
        and Company, 1985.

        The individual studies in this book provide a historical
background that helps to understand women's position in Tanzania
today.   The focus is on the rural sector and the lowest-paid
workers in towns.   The conclusion of the book indicates that
women have two possibilities: 1) they may be driven into a
position in which they subject themselves to continued hardship and
suffering, or 2) women can take matters into their own hands and
gain more power. *(See 160)*.

232.   Swantz, Marja-Liisa. "The Effect of Economic Change on
        Gender Roles: The Case of Tanzania." Development (SID)
        2-3 (1988): 93-96.

        Focuses on the case of Tanzania to discuss the rapid change
in the African economy and its impact on women.   Shows the
central role women play in reproducing their households and the
economy.   Suggests how government policies need to support
women's self-initiated economic activities.   The context is specific
to Tanzania, but the issues raised have relevance for developing
countries in general. *(See 176, 231, 234)*.

233.   Tadesse, Zenebworke.   "Bringing Research Home."
        Development: Seeds of Change 4 (1984): 50-54.

        Provides a critical review of research on women in Africa.
For the most part, this research is carried out by outsiders. It is
only since 1977, with the foundation of the Association of African
Women for Research, that women's issues are being seriously
addressed by Africans themselves.

234.   Tripp, Aili Mari.   "Women and the Changing Urban
        Household Economy in Tanzania." Journal of Modern
        African Studies 27, no. 4 (Dec 1989): 601-623.

        Attempts to analyze the responses of women to the

economic hardships in Tanzania, where women became increasingly involved in the informal sector of the economy and generated their own income. This gave them more power in the household and improved their situation. *(See 184, 232).*

235.   Walker, Cherryl. Women and Resistance in South Africa. London: Onyx Press, 1982.

This book provides a valuable addition to the written history of South African politics and gives a detailed account of women's involvement in 20th century political struggles. It charts the rise and fall of the Federation of South African women and women's roles in other political organizations. *(See 221, 602, 604).*

236.   Watts, Susan J. "Rural Women as Food Processors and Traders: Eko Making in the Ilorin Area of Nigeria." Journal of Developing Areas 19, no. 1 (October 1984): 71-82.

Many women in West Africa are petty traders and are economically independent. This study focuses on the processing and selling of a maize-meal snack, eko, by rural women in the city of Ilorin, Nigeria. It discusses the production-trading hierarchy and shows that lack of education or capital prevents traders from taking advantage of lucrative opportunities. Suggests that Third World planners encourage traditional trading activities by women in order to enhance economic development. *(See 159, 163).*

Chapter Three

Asia

3.1 Women of Asia: An Introduction

237.   Aguilar, Delia M. "Women in the Political Economy of the Philippines." Alternatives 12, no. 4 (October 1987): 511-526.

Argues that the oppression of women in Filipino society cannot be isolated from the oppressive character of the society. The Philippines provides a clear example of how that nation's colonial past and neocolonial present affect Filipino women's lives today. It is by viewing the society in its entirety that the author explains the sale of the bodies of women, mail-order brides, migrant women workers and their below-subsistence wages. *(See 250, 254, 280, 313, 319, 619).*

238.   Allen, Michael, and S.N. Mukherjee (eds.). Women in India and Nepal. New York: Apts Books, Inc., 1990.

This Collection of essays addresses some of the major contradictions in women's lives and helps us understand the seeming paradoxes in the social life of women in India and Nepal. *(See 240, 242, 330).*

239.   Ariffin, Rohana. "The Exploitation of Women: An Overview." SOJOURN 1, no. 2 (August 1986): 133-54.

Discusses the position of women in Malaysia and attempts to explain the factors which contribute to women's exploitation, both in the public and private spheres. *(See 251, 273, 554, 580).*

240.   Bennett, Lynn. Women, Poverty, and Productivity in India. Washington, D.C.: The World Bank, 1992.

This publication looks at the effect of gender on access within the family and beyond. It is based on the World Banks's 1991 study of women's involvement in key sectors of the Indian economy, and the benefits and constraints that they face in these sectors. *(See 238, 241, 244, 253, 288, 582, 622).*

241.   Burra, Neera. "Out of Sight, Out of Mind: Working Girls in India." International Labour Review 128, no. 5 (1989): 651-660.

There is a significant difference between the situation of working girls and that of working boys in India. This article discusses the variety of ways this difference expresses itself. An enlightening article which shows the dark side of children's lives, in general, and girls' lives, in particular. *(See 238, 286, 408).*

242.   Chiang, Lan-hung. "The New Social and Economic Roles of Chinese Women in Taiwan and Their Implications for Policy and Development." Journal of Developing Societies 5, no. 1 (January-April 1989): 96-106.

Examines women's educational attainment and economic participation in recent decades. Women's roles have changed, but they remain ghettoized in certain types of work. Major social policies are needed to ensure women's full participation in the labour force. *(See 261, 265, 293, 302).*

243.   Croll, Elizabeth. Chinese Women Since Mao. London: Zed Press, 1983.

The author examines the repercussions of China's new policies on the role and status of women in post-Mao China. The implications for women are often not clear. This book is of particular use for those interested in understanding the consequences of socialist modernization in China, for women. *(See 252, 613).*

244.   Dandekar, Hemalata C. "Indian Women's Development: Four Lenses." South Asia Bulletin 6, no. 1 (Spring 1986): 25-29.

Stresses the complex and heterogeneous nature of Indian women's needs and aspirations. Uses four interdependent aspects of women's lives: the economic and work; the public realm; the family structure; and attitudes toward women, to understand women's place in society. The framework developed here is useful not only for studying women in India, but women in Third World countries as a whole. *(See 240, 241, 626).*

245.   Khaing, Mimi. The World of Burmese Women. London: Zed Books, 1984.

The author provides a portrait of Burmese women in all spheres of life: women's status, women in the family, women in the rural and urban areas, women and religion. She concludes that Burmese women are less differentiated against and oppressed than elsewhere. *(See 249, 346).*

246.   Matsui, Yayori. Women's Asia. London: Zed Books, 1989.

The author draws on her experience in seventeen Asian countries and shows the daily challenges faced by women from many different classes and cultures. This book shows Asian women in their diversity, their subordination and their courage. *(See 281, 303, 306, 348).*

247.   Pandi, Harshida. Women in India: An Annotated Bibliography. New York: Garland Publishing company, 1985.

The focus is on women's status in India, and the bibliography provides a long list of studies on various aspects of women's lives in India.

248.   Rozario, Santi. Purity and Communal Boundaries: Women and Social Change in a Bangladeshi Village. London: Zed Books, 1992.

This book discusses the status of women in the context of drastic socioeconomic changes. It analyses the interaction between communal, gender and class hierarchy in the Bangladeshi village of Doria, comprised of a Muslim, Hindu and Christian population. *(See 276, 279, 290, 300, 622).*

249.   Skjonsberg, Else. A Special Caste: Tamil Women of Sri Lanka. London: Zed Press, 1982.

The author focuses on the complex inter-relations between sex, caste and class that shape the lives of Tamil women. She argues that these women labour under the burden of triple oppression. *(See 245, 321).*

250.   Uy Eviota, Elizabeth. The Political Economy of Gender: Women and the Sexual Division of Labour in the Philippines. London: Zed Books, 1992.

The author explores the intersection between gender ideology and the sexual division of labour. She shows that women are concentrated in certain types of occupations, and focuses on the changing position of women in the labour market. She also provides a critical account of the literature on women. *(See 237, 280).*

251.   Ward, Colleen. "Women and Community Development in Malaysia: The Kanita Project." Women's Studies International Forum 5, no. 1 (1982): 99-101.

Discusses the Kanita Project, which investigated women's multiple roles in the Malaysian economy. This project can serve as an example for promoting rural development in developing countries. *(See 239, 273, 301,625).*

252.   Wolf, Margery.   Revolution Postponed: Women in Contemporary China. Stanford: Stanford University Press, 1985.

The author looks at change and continuity in women's lives in China since the Revolution and shows the extent to which women's tasks as mother/wife remain unchallenged. *(See 243, 263, 290, 315, 355, 615, 627).*

3.2 The Social Construction of Gender

253.   Afshar, Haleh, and Bina Agarwal (ed.). Women, Poverty and Ideology in Asia: Contradictory Pressures, Uneasy Resolutions. London: Macmillan, 1989.

This collection brings together issues concerning a mixed set of Asian countries, with an associated diversity of cultural and economic conditions. They cover a wide range of ideologies: the ideology of seclusion and exclusion; and the social construction of femininity and demarcation of roles by gender. All of these affect the way women attempt to earn a living. *(See 240, 500).*

254.   Aguilar, Delia D. "The Social Construction of the Filipino Woman." International Journal of Intercultural Relations 13, no. 4 (1989): 527-51.

Criticizes social science for its construction of Filipino women.   Credits women and development literature for demystifying women's status in the public domain but stresses that understanding of women's role in the family still remains obscure. *(See 237).*

255.   Charyulu, U.V.N., and G. Narayana Reddy.   "Rural Women: Decision-Making, Public Participation and Other Basic Needs: A Study of Two South Indian Villages."

Indian Journal of Social Work 47, no. 4 (January 1987):
407-415.

This study is based on a survey of two villages in India. It
shows that patriarchal and semi-feudal ideologies dominate the
social structures in these villages and are the obstacles towards
women's emancipation.   It suggests that efforts should be
concentrated on raising women's awareness of their roles in
society. *(See 238, 240).*

256.   Coomaraswamy, Radhika.   "The Impact of Tradition,
        Culture and Religion on Women in South Asia." Ethnic
        Studies Report 6, no. 2 (July 1988): 65-84.

Criticizes the unilinear approach to development and social
change for being inadequate for understanding the persistent
dynamics of religion and culture in Asian societies. Women's
empowerment would not be possible without addressing the values
inherent in the social institutions which legitimize women's unequal
position. Highlights the significant role that religion and tradition
play in women's lives. *(See 168).*

257.   Devendra, Kiran. Status and Position of Women in India:
        With Special Reference to Women in Contemporary India.
        New Delhi: Shakti Books, 1985.

This book looks at the changes brought about in the position
of Indian women since 1974. While it is possible for women to
adopt a career and the law has also given them protection, the
environment both at home and in the society, has not changed
much. The changes that have taken place are more apparent than
real. *(See 258, 617).*

258.   Dhruvarajan, Vanaja. Hindu Women and the Power of
        Ideology. Mass.: Bergin and Garvey Publishers Inc.,
        1989.

This monograph inquires into the life of Hindu women.
The author's quest is to understand how women are made to accept

legitimacy of their subordinate position. *(See 257, 272).*

259. Eden, Joseph A.   "Life Cycle Strategies of Female
      Assembly Line Workers in Malaysia: Demographic Profiles
      of a Dual Work Force." Urban Anthropology 18, no. 2
      (Summer 1989): 153-185.

      Uses the cases of the semiconductor and garment industries
to show the importance of ethnic and labour ideology in the labour
process. Ethnicity is used as a tactic to ensure a fluid supply of
labour. *(See 239, 251).*

260. Engineer, Asghar Ali (ed.).   Status of Women in Islam.
      Delhi: A Janta Publications, 1987.

      This book is an honest attempt to shed light on women's
status in Islam from theological, political, and sociological points
of view. The articles in this book make a plausible case for equal
status for women and deal with the dynamics of change. *(See 165,
275, 469, 471, 618).*

261. Gallin, Rita S.   "Women, Family and the Political
      Economy of Taiwan." Journal of Peasant Studies 12, no.
      1 (Oct. 1984): 76-92.

      The traditional Chinese family system fosters values and
behaviours necessary for the development of capitalism in Taiwan.
The state encourages patriarchal familialism which justifies its
employment practices and the existing underdeveloped social
security system. *(See 242, 265, 293, 310).*

262. Hale, Sylvia M. "Male Culture and Purdah for Women:
      The Social Construction of What Women Think."
      Canadian Review of Sociology and Anthropology 25, no.
      2 (May 1988): 276-98.

      This case study of rural India questions the concept of
dominant culture.   It shows the discrepancies between the
normative patterns of female behaviour and what women actually

do in concrete choice situations. It concludes that only male perspectives have become rigidified as the collective experience of the community as a whole, without women being consulted. *(See 260, 469, 471)*.

263.   Hemmel, Vibeke, and Pia Sindbjerg. Women in Rural China: Policy Towards Women Before and After the Cultural Revolution. London: Curzon Press Ltd., 1984.

This book concentrates on the official attitude towards the role of women in China. It examines the extent to which women's position has changed under Socialist China. *(See 243, 252, 613)*.

264.   Jayaweera, Swarna. "Gender and Access to Education in Asia." International Review of Education 33, no. 4 (1987): 455-66.

Discusses the social and economic constraints which prevent women from having equal access to education. This is particularly true for six Asian countries where patriarchal structures compound other barriers and increase gender disparities in educational participation. *(See 376, 473, 512)*.

265.   Kung, Lydia. Factory Women in Taiwan. Ann Arbor: UMI Research Press, 1983.

This book provides a background on women and work in traditional Chinese society and shows the importance of ideology in this regard. It looks at the process of integration into the industrial labour force and the relationship between work, family and factory life. It demonstrates the complex interaction between women's status, the family, and the national and international economy. *(See 242, 261, 293, 302, 338, 573)*.

266.   Levidow, Les. "Women Who Make the Chips." Science as Culture 2, no. 1 (1991): 103-124.

The development of technology facilitated the internationalization of capital and labour. In search of cheap labour, computer chip manufacturers make use of women's labour. This study shows that Malay women, who are controlled by the ideologies of capitalism and Islam are a major source of cheap labour. *(See 271, 274, 418, 420).*

267. Mahajan, Amarjit. "Status of Thai Women: A Socio-Historical Analysis." Guru Nanak Journal of Sociology 8, no. 1 (April 1987): 154-60.

A general discussion which shows that in Thailand, as in many other places, women's role as wives and mothers is emphasized. Shows that historically and culturally, there has been an emphasis on the gendered division of labour. *(See 274, 316, 633, 634).*

268. Massanari, Ronald L. "Sexual Imagery and Religion: An Intercultural Exploration. The Linga-Yoni and Temples at Khajuraho." Journal of Gender in World Religions 2, (1991): 1-13.

Acknowledges religious pluralism and stresses the uniqueness of each religion's tradition. Deals with the question of sexuality in the Hindu religion. Through this focus, provides inter-religious dialogue. *(See 469).*

269. McAllister, Carol. "Women and Feasting: Ritual Exchange, Capitalism, and Islamic Revival in Negeri Sembilan, Malaysia." Research in Economic Anthropology 12 (1990): 23-51.

Examines the importance of feasting as a means for non-market exchange. Shows the centrality of women in the communal feast, and the persistence of this complex ritual in a period of capitalist development. Focuses on the fate of this system of ritual exchange during Malaysia's growing participation in the global economy. *(See 256).*

270. McDonough, Sheila. "Yusuf Ali and Mawdudi on Gender in the Qur'an." Journal of Gender in World Religions 2

(1991):15-36.

Focuses on the writings of two widely-read Indian authors
(Yusuf Ali and Mawlana Mawdudi) and their different
interpretations of the Qur'an. Raises important questions regarding
Muslim women's rights and the interpretation of justice. *(See
260).*

271.   Mies, M.   The Lace Makers of Narsapur: Indian
       Housewives Produce for the World Market. London: Zed
       Press, 1982.

This study demonstrates the interplay between caste, class
and gender. Women lace makers experience discrimination in the
labour market. Their notion of what is appropriate for women
prevents them from taking on any work which would remove their
isolated status as housewives. *(See 19, 137, 266, 307, 418, 420,
657).*

272.   Mitter, Sara S. Dharma's Daughters: Contemporary Indian
       Women and Hindu Culture.   New Jersey: Rutgers
       University Press, 1991.

This book examines the lives of contemporary Indian
women and looks at women who work and live in the cities. It
discusses the impact of the Hindu myth in reproducing women's
position and reveals that women have shown growing resistance
since the 1970s. *(See 258).*

273.   Nasir, Rohany. "Sex-Role Attitudes of Malaysian Women:
       Implications for Career Development and Counselling."
       SOJOURN 1, no. 2 (August 1986): 172-82.

This study compares the sex-role attitudes of three groups
of women in Malaysia: 1) women in non-traditional careers, 2)
women in traditional jobs, and 3) home-maker women. The results
show that there are significant differences among these women.
(See 239, 251).

274.   Porpora, Douglas V., Mah Hui Lim, and Usanee Prommas.
        "The Role of Women in the International Division of
        Labour: The Case of Thailand." Development and Change
        20, no. 2 (April 1989): 269-294.

        The data for this paper, which come from interviews with
management and workers of textile industries in Thailand, show
that low-paying jobs are being relocated to developing countries.
It argues that management prefers female workers, not because
they are more docile, but because such work has traditionally been
performed by women. *(See 269, 271, 418, 420, 632, 633).*

275.   Quintos R. C. Lily. "Women and Culture: Women's
        Struggle for Equality in Church and Society." Impact 24,
        no. 7 (July 1989): 18-27.

        Discusses the sociocultural and historical process of
women's subordination in three Asian cultures: Japan, Indonesia,
and the Philippines. Regardless of differences in religion, women
had to struggle to gain equality. In each of the cases discussed,
women's subordination was sustained and legitimized through the
complex interplay of social, economic and ideological factors.
Calls for change in social and religious paradigms in order to
achieve equality for women. *(See 260, 480).*

276.   Rauf, Abdur. "Rural Women and the Family: A Study of
        a Punjabi Village in Pakistan." Journal of Comparative
        Family Studies 18, no. 3 (Autumn 1987): 403-15.

        This paper discusses some of the structural constraints that
affect the status of women in Pakistan. While some changes are
evident in the rural areas, the current attitudes are such that they
have perpetuated the image of women as 'dependent' persons.
(See 248, 358, 618).

3.3 Women, State and Development Policies

277.   Abdullah, Noraini. "Women and Politics of the State."

SOJOURN 2 (August 1986): 213-19.

This article makes a strong case that the Malaysian State is involved in the endorsement and enforcement of a gender ideology that subordinates women. *(See 27).*

278.   Alva, Margaret. "Women, the Vital Human Resource." Development (SID) 2-3 (1988): 53-55.

The author is Minister for Women and Child Development in India. Describes some of the actions taken by the government in promoting women's position and acknowledges the importance of women in the productive and reproductive spheres. It concludes that rights and equality for women lie not in amending the laws, but in their implementation. *(See 2, 22, 282).*

279.   Begum, Kohinoor. "Participation of Rural Women in Income-Earning Activities: A Case Study of a Bangladesh Village." Women's Studies International Forum 12, no. 5 (1989): 519-528.

This case study of a rural village in Bangladesh demonstrates the multiple role of women in the household and in the economy at large. Despite women's central place in the economy and in the household, development projects are influenced by norms and values which subtly deny their full participation. Moreover, in this process, the lower status women are the ones who become even more marginalized. *(See 248, 329).*

280.   Bello, Walden, David Kinley, and Elaine Elinson. Development Debacle: The World Bank in the Philippines. San Francisco: Institute for Food and Development Policy, 1982.

This publication critically examines the World Bank's projects in the Philippines and argues that these projects have had a negative impact. The result has been more hunger, more foreign control over resources and more political dictatorship. *(See 237, 250, 254, 569).*

281. Blumberg, Rae Lesser, and Cara Hinderstein. "At the End of the Line: Women and United States Foreign Aid in Asia, 1978-1980." Women and Politics 2, no. 4 (Winter 1982): 43-66).

Evaluates four of USAID's projects which focus on women. Most projects do not even mention women. Suggests that women's interests are more likely to be present if they are among the members of the study team. *(See 246, 378).*

282. Chen, Marty. "A Sectoral Approach to Promoting Women's Work: Lessons from India." World Development 17, no. 7 (July 1989): 1007-1016.

Attempts to promote women's position in development. Suggests that applying a sectoral framework to the analysis of women's work may provide a way to close the gap between the now well-documented economic roles of women and the, as yet, male-biased macro-economic planning done by governments. Uses the case of India for citing the success of such an approach. *(See 278, 349).*

283. Ling, Chee Yoke. "Women, Environment and Development: The Malaysian Experience." Development (SID) 2-3 (1989): 88-91.

The three case studies in this paper show the negative impact that growth based on material gain has had on women and the environment in Malaysia. Environmental protection and the health impact of the increasing use of chemicals in agriculture have been neglected. Cash crop production has reduced women's control over land and food production. *(See 5, 21).*

284. Palileo, Gloria J. "Rural Development and Women's Economic Roles in Asia." International Review of Modern Sociology 17, no. 2 (Autumn 1987): 297-312.

Attempts to find the extent to which the role of rural women will change as a result of development programs.

Identifies a number of factors that affect the role of rural women and examines the impact of six types of development activities on women. *(See 130)*.

285.   Pollock, Nancy J.   "The Early Development of Housekeeping and Imports in Fiji." Pacific Studies 12, no. 2 (March 1989): 53-82.

Evaluates the impact of British missionary women on various aspects of women's lives in Fiji.   Refers to these missionary women as the "first development agents,"and argues that the patterns they have established have become a liability.

286.   Sachs, Carolyn E.   "Women, Minorities, and Children as Special Targets of Development in Third World Nations." International Journal of Contemporary Sociology 24, nos. 3-4 (July- October 1987): 113-126.

Development programs have worsened the situation of women, children, and minorities. In the short-term, policies are needed to enhance their access to resources. In the long-term, the process of development itself must be altered to improve their situation. *(See 241, 408)*.

287.   Srinivasan, Shobha.   Breaking Rural Bonds Through Migration: The Failure of Development for Women in India. Ph.D. Thesis. Chicago: Loyola University, 1989.

Examines how development affects women. Argues that discounted, discriminated against, deprived and debilitated, India's women carry the brunt of the poverty burden. *(See 10, 130, 284, 611)*.

288.   Tendler, Judith.   "What Ever Happened to Poverty Alleviation?" World Development 17, no. 7 (July 1989): 1033-44.

Points to the failure of many development programs directed toward alleviating poverty. Evaluates the characteristics

of several programs funded by the Ford Foundation, and suggests
a number of recommendations to enable donor agencies to improve
their programs. *(See 240, 253, 582, 626, 637).*

289.   Varma, Sudhir. "Policy Planning for Women's
        Development at Provincial Level-The Case of Rajasthan."
        Development (SID) 1 (1990): 95-98.

Uses information on one of the most underdeveloped
provinces in India to show that there has not been a serious attempt
to respond administratively to the suggestions made by the UN
regarding women. Policy planning has been gender-blind and
women have been ignored. For women to truly be part of the
development process, women's issues should be integrated into all
levels of State policies--local and national. *(See 10, 130).*

290.   Weeks, Margaret R. "Virtuous Wives and Kind Mothers:
        Concepts of Women in Urban China." Women's Studies
        International Forum 12, no. 5 (1989): 505-18.   .

Discusses the major social and structural problems that
hinder women from achieving equality in China. Argues that
forty years of socialism have done little to challenge patriarchal
attitudes. Class, instead of gender, was given priority. Therefore,
many of the attitudes which accounted for the subordination of
women continue to exist. *(See 33, 252, 300, 326, 355).*

3.4 Work and Family

291.   Alam, Sultana. "Women and Poverty in Bangladesh."
        Women's Studies International Forum 8, no. 4 (1985): 361-
        71.

Uses qualitative data to discuss the rise of female-headed
households in Bangladesh. Shows that the increase in the number
of single women is not a sign of liberation, but of the abandonment
of women. *(See 253, 279, 622).*

292.   Bennett, Lynn.   Dangerous Wives and Sacred Sisters:
       Social and Symbolic Roles of High-Caste Women in Nepal.
       New York: Columbia University Press, 1983.

This book examines the way in which the social roles of
high-caste Nepali women combine to define their position in the
patriarchal Hindu society.   It shows that women's social roles in
Hindu kinship and family structures are related to their symbolic
role in the ritual of Hinduism.   Hindu women cannot be
understood in isolation from the Hindu culture.   *(See 238, 290,
297)*.

293.   Greenhalgh, Susan.   "Sexual Stratification: The Other Side
       of 'Growth with Equity' in East Asia."   Population and
       Development Review 11, no. 2 (June 1985): 265-314.

Explores changes in women's status in Taiwan and argues
that rapid economic development has intensified and reinforced the
traditional sexual stratification.   The patriarchal family structure
supports traditional sexual hierarchies.   The task is to implement
policies which question the subordinate status of women.   *(See
242, 261, 265)*.

294.   Johnson, Kay Ann.   Women, The Family and Peasant
       Revolution in China. Chicago: The University of Chicago
       Press, 1983.

This book examines the policies and changes concerning
women that developed in the rural areas under the Chinese
Communist Party during both the revolutionary and post-
revolutionary periods.   The primary focus is on the reform of
marriage and the family.   *(See 243, 252, 630)*.

295.   Johnson, Patricia Lyons.   "Women and Development: A
       Highland New Guinea Example."   Human Ecology 16, no.
       2 (June 1988): 105-122.

Evaluates households' success in cash cropping in New
Guinea.   Illustrates that the number of female residents, including

wives, has a direct impact on production. In addition to their domestic work, women are involved in commercial and non-domestic production. *(See 114, 359).*

296.   Noponen, Helzi Tuula. The Gender Division of Labor in the Urban Informal Sector of Developing Countries: A Panel Survey of Households in Madras, India. Ph.D. diss., University of California, Berkeley, 1988.

Demonstrates the pivotal role that women's earnings play in the welfare and survival of poor households. In a large number of the households, women have the primary income earning role. Among the poorer segment of the urban population, women's earnings are not supplementary but rather are sustaining, providing the family income without which the family would fall below the poverty line. *(See 10, 178, 365, 407, 419).*

297.   Panter-Brick, Catherine. "Motherhood and Subsistence Work: The Tamang of Rural Nepal." Human Ecology 17, no. 2 (June 1989): 205-28.

The author examines the type of work and work patterns of Nepalese women of different child-bearing statuses and the extent to which their participation is modified during pregnancy. Reveals important details about women's work in Nepal and shows that during times of high demand for labour, women's responsibilities are hardly modified during pregnancy. This, of course, has an impact on women and their children's health. *(See 238, 292).*

298.   Reeves, Joy B. "Work and Family Roles: Contemporary Women in Indonesia." Sociological Spectrum 7, no. 3 (1986): 223-42.

Looks at family-work integration and compares the U.S. with Indonesia. Concludes that there is less sex-based stratification in Indonesia than in the U.S. Women in Indonesia can also achieve family-work integration relatively easier than in the U.S. As Indonesia develops economically, it is predicted that we will see the growth of sex-based stratification. *(See 317, 341, 629).*

299.   Tan, Thomas T. W., and Theresa W. Devasahayam.
        "Opposition and Interdependence: The Dialectics of Maid
        and Employer Relationships in Singapore." Philippine
        Sociological Review 35, nos. 3-4 (July-December 1987):
        34-41.

        Focuses on the influx of immigrant maids to Singapore.
Suggests that Filipino domestic workers' temporary movement to
Singapore can be understood within the framework provided by
world system theory. Sheds light on social relations and the
interaction among maids and their employers and helps us to
understand the cultural patterns which contribute to the
reproduction of such relationships. *(See 198)*.

3.5 Women's Experience of Wage-work

300.   Amin, A. T. M. Nurul. "The Role of the Informal Sector
        in Economic Development: Some Evidence from Dhaka,
        Bangladesh." International Labour Review 126, no. 5
        (September-October. 1987): 611-23.

        The informal sector plays a major part in the economy of
Bangladesh. It provides an employment opportunity to rural
migrants who are pushed out of agriculture. The attention of
policy makers needs to be drawn to this vastly expanding sector.
(See 248, 279, 290).

301.   Armstrong, M. Jocelyn. "Women's Friendships under
        Urbanization: A Malaysian Study." Women's Studies
        International Forum 10, no. 6 (1987): 623-633.

        This paper is based on field research on white collar women
in Kuala Lumpur, Malaysia. The aim is to discover how white
collar women find friendship and support systems in an urban area.
The strategies of recruitment and maintenance of friendship are
discussed. By being placed in an urban environment and away
from kin, women are exposed to non-traditional values and develop
cross-ethnic friendships. *(See 8, 239, 251, 625)*.

302.   Arrigo, Linda Gail. "Economic and Political Control of
        Women Workers in Multinational Electronics Factories in
        Taiwan: Martial Law Coercion and World Market
        Uncertainty." Contemporary Marxism 11 (Fall 1985): 77-
        95.

        Analyses women's work and their position in the export
processing zones of Taiwan. Shows the role of the State and the
coercive methods used in controlling labour. *(See 242, 261, 265).*

303.   Binswanger, H. P., et.al. (eds.) Rural Household Studies
        in Asia. Singapore: Singapore University Press, 1980.

        The basic building block of economies--households--are
usually neglected in large-scale economic analysis. In this volume
the authors present a comprehensive study of the household,
bringing to light the link between individual household behavior
and production of the State and the larger economy. Women and
other household members play a central role in the production and
reproduction of the households. *(See 315, 326, 330).*

304.   Chaudhary, S. N., and Pratima Chaudhary. "Some
        Problems of Home-Based Piece-Rate Women Workers."
        Indian Journal of Social Work 50, no. 3 (July 1989): 263-
        70.

        This paper discusses the types of piecework that women do
in India and identifies the problems that female pieceworkers face.
Provides suggestions for policy makers and solutions for improving
women's working conditions. *(See 115, 240).*

305.   Christian Conference of Asia-Urban Rural Mission (CCA-
        URM). Struggling to Survive: Women Workers in Asia.
        Hong Kong: CCA-URM, 1981.

        This book provides a general and short overview of women
workers in five Asian countries. Women in these countries have
many similarities, but bear the distinctiveness of their local
situations. *(See 246, 281).*

306.   Chung, Yuen Kay. "Negotiating Target": An Ethnographic
        Exploration of Women and Work in a High Technology
        Factory in Singapore." Studies in Sexual Politics 23
        (1988): 1-89.

        This paper is based on the author's Ph.D. thesis and focuses
on women workers in a multinational industry. It argues that
women act in organized ways, like men, to achieve desired goals.
"Femininity" and "passivity" are accomplishments used to gain
power in the workplace. (See 3, 176, 578).

307.   Committee for Asian Women. The Plight of Asian Women
        in Electronics. Kowloon, Hong Kong: Christian Conference
        of Asia-Urban Rural Mission (CCA-URM), 1982.

        This book explores the working conditions of women
workers in the electronics industry, which in the 1970s entered the
mainstream of the world's top industrial producers. It provides
much information on electronics industries, government
involvement, and women's response to their situation. (See 271,
308, 418).

308.   Deyo, Frederic C. (ed.). The Political Economy of the
        New Asian Industrialism. Ithaca: Cornell University Press,
        1987.

        This collection of essays explores the Asian Newly
Industrialized Countries' (NICs) exceptional ability to capitalize on
the favourable economic environment of the 1960s, and then to
adapt flexibly to worsening conditions in the 1970s and 1980s.
Together, the essays seek to discuss forces which account for the
success of State-led export-oriented industrialization. (See 266,
274, 628).

309.   Feldman, Shelley, and Florence E. McCarthy. "Conditions
        Influencing Rural and Town Women's Participation in the
        Labor   Force: Some   Important   Considerations."
        International Journal of Intercultural Relations 6, no. 4
        (1982): 421-40.

Suggests that economic difficulties forced women into wage-work. The expansion of the wage economy has not brought more equality for women, but has changed the form of inequality and exploitation. The Western model of development brought new forms of control and contradictory results. *(See 6, 29, 31).*

310. Gallin, Rita S. "The Entry of Chinese Women into the Rural Labour Force: A Case Study from Taiwan." Signs 9, no. 3 (Spring 1984): 383-98.

Discusses the impact of economic development on women's work and status in Taiwan. Women entered the public sector and engaged in agricultural work, however, social and legal changes did not enhance women's authority. Traditional values persist as they are congruent with the political economy of contemporary Taiwan. *(See 242, 261, 265).*

311. Grossman, Rachael. "Women's Place in the Integrated Circuit." Radical America 14, no. 1 (January-February 1980): 29-49.

The production process of which the semi-conductor factories in Southeast Asia are a part is literally a global assembly line stretching more than halfway around the world. This industry requires an expendable workforce and women constitute such workers. *(See 266, 420).*

312. Heyzer, Noeleen. "Asian Women Wage-Earners: Their Situation and Possibilities for Donor Intervention." World Development 17, no. 7 (July 1989): 1109-23.

Argues that industrialization and modernization have worsened the economic position of women. Suggests that donor institutions and development policy-makers give priority to low-income women in order to break the chain of poverty. *(See 2, 113).*

313. Iyori, Naoko. "Asian Women Against Sexual Slavery." Migration World 14, nos. 1-2 (1986): 44-45.

Focuses on Filipino immigrant women in Japan who are employed as what have come to be known as "entertainers." Discusses the slavery and exploitative relationship involved in this type of work. Deals with the mechanisms involved in the traffic of women as sexual entertainers. *(See 237, 319, 324).*

314.   Judd, Ellen.   "Alternative Development Strategies for Women in Rural China." Development and Change 21, no. 1 (January. 1990): 23-42.

This study is based on ethnographic research in three villages in Shandong Province during 1986 and 1987-88. It examines women's participation in productive labour outside the household. Women play a major role in rural development by working in agriculture, rural industry, and household-based production units. *(See 252, 333).*

315.   Korabik, Karen.   "Women at Work in China: The Struggle for Equality in a Changing Society." Resources for Feminist Research 16, no. 4 (December 1987): 33-34.

Uses observation and interviews to compare the experience of working women in China with that in Western countries. Concludes that patriarchal views continue to force women into inferior positions in the labour market. Recent reforms have both helped and hindered women's position. *(See 252, 290, 331).*

316.   Lockwood, Victoria Joralemon.   "Capitalist Development and the Socioeconomic Position of Tahitian Peasant Women." Journal of Anthropological Research 44, no. 3 (Fall 1988): 263-85.

Uses the case of Tahitian peasant women to show how the penetration of capitalism promotes female economic subordination within the commodity-producing households. In contrast, in precontact society women possessed high social status, economic and political power, and personal autonomy. *(See 267, 274, 632, 633).*

317.   Mather, Celia E.   "Industrialization in the Tangerang
        Regency of West Java: Women Workers and the Islamic
        Patriarchy." Bulletin of Concerned Asian Scholars 15, no.
        2 (1983): 2-17.

        Looks at the social impact of industrialization in West Java.
The alliance of capitalist and patriarchal Islamic ideology
reinforced the subordination of women as daughters, wives, and
mothers. Industrial capital benefitted from the cheap labour of
young people, especially women. *(See 298, 325, 327, 554).*

318.   Mies, Maria. "Capitalism and Subsistence: Rural Women
        in India." Development: Seeds of Change 4 (1984): 18-24.

        Analyses   pauperization,   marginalization,   and   the
deteriorating status of women in India within the context of
capitalist development and accumulation. Argues that the fight
against sexism must become an integral part of any struggle to
eliminate class rule. *(See 19, 271).*

319.   O'Malley, Jeff.   "Sex Tourism and Women's Status in
        Thailand." Loisir et Société/Society and Leisure 11, no. 1
        (printemps 1988): 99-114.

        Identifies a series of economic, social, and political
conditions which account for both the large scale and exploitative
nature of the Thai sex-tourism industry. In the face of high
unemployment, women use this channel of work to support their
families. *(See 237, 313, 324).*

320.   Ong, Aihwa.   Spirits of Resistance and Capitalist
        Discipline: Factory Women in Malaysia. Albany: State
        University of New York Press, 1987.

        Argues that capitalist development in Malaysia engenders
new forms of discipline in the everyday life of Malays, who, up to
recently, were largely rooted in village society and engaged in
small-scale cash cropping. Explores how changing relationships in
the peasant household, village, and global factory mediate

divergent attitudes towards work and sexuality among Malays and within the wider society. *(See 19, 221, 301)*.

321.   Perera, H. E. Myrtle. "The Changing Status of Women in Sri Lanka." International Journal of Sociology of the Family 17, no. 1 (Spring 1987): 1-23.

Discusses the impact of modernization on the position of women in Sri Lanka. In this case, the overriding element appears to be a question of reconciling traditional value systems and the equality of rights and status as spelled out by the global ideals of the modern woman. Brings out very clearly, the conflicts between the demands of traditional and modern values regarding women and development. *(See 249, 499)*.

322.   Ram, Kalpana. Mukkuvar Women: Gender, Hegemony and Capitalist Transformation in a South Indian Fishing Community. London: Zed Books, 1991.

This book is a study of social change and capitalist transformation in fishing communities. The author argues that far from involving women in the wider social network of production and exchange, capitalism has narrowed the horizons of women's working lives. *(See 19, 271)*.

323.   Shaw, Annapurna. "Linkages of Large Scale, Small Scale and Informal Sector Industries: A Study of Thana-Belapur." Economic and Political Weekly (February 17-24, 1990): M-17-M-22.

Argues that the process of industrialization in India is complex. Capital-intensive, large-scale industrial units and small-scale industries co-exist with the informal sector. These units operate simultaneously and this paper analyses linkages among them. Provides empirical evidence for the importance of a linkage between the formal and informal sectors of the economy in the Third World. *(See 8, 178)*.

324.   Tan, Michael, Adul de Leon, Brenda Stoltzfus, and Cindy

O'Donnell. "AIDS as a Political Issue: Working with the Sexually Prostituted in the Philippines." Community Development Journal 24, no. 3 (July 1989): 186-193.

Discusses the problems that face women who are involved in prostitution. Government's tourism policies and U.S. military bases are seen as the major determinants of issues related to the so-called "hospitality women." Outlines the difficulties associated with preventative AIDS educational programs. *(See 237, 313, 319).*

325.   White, Mary C. "Improving the Welfare of Women Factory Workers: Lessons from Indonesia." International Labour Review 129, no. 1 (1990): 121-33.

Women have become an integral part of economic development in Indonesia. However, they remain concentrated in low-level occupations. This article calls for an improvement in women's working conditions. Sheds light on our knowledge of women and factory work, in general. *(See 298, 317).*

326.   Wilson-Moore, Margot. "Women's Work in Homestead Gardens: Subsistence, Patriarchy, and Status in Northwest Bangladesh." Urban Anthropology 18, nos. 3-4 (Fall-Winter 1989): 281-297.

Provides a review of the feminist critique of development theory and uses the case study of a village in Bangladesh to demonstrate that women's economic contributions do not necessarily lead to an improvement in their socioeconomic status. For development programs to affect women positively, they must focus on the needs of women. *(See 248, 291).*

327.   Wolf, Diane L. "Daughters, Decisions and Domination: An Empirical and Conceptual Critique of Household Strategies." Development and Change 21, no. 1 (January 1990): 43-74.

Focuses on women and their households in Java and

Taiwan. Analyses the decision-making process in the family with regard to young women and factory employment, and critically evaluates the extent to which these processes reflect family strategy. *(See 242, 317).*

328.   Wong, Aline K.   "Planned Development, Social Stratification, and the Sexual Division of Labour in Singapore." Signs 7, no. 2 (Winter 1981): 434-52.

Discusses the economic development in Singapore and shows its dependent nature. This development did not alter the sexual division of labour, but expanded employment opportunities for women. As well, it has brought women into particular types of jobs which are characterized by lower status and low pay. *(See 271, 318).*

3.6 Working in the Rural Areas

329.   Abdullah, Tahrunnessa A., and Sondra A. Zeidenstein. Village Women of Bangladesh: Prospect for Change and Study. Oxford: Pergamon Press, 1982.

This book describes and evaluates an attempt in Bangladesh to increase incomes of rural households by the establishment of self-directed credit co-operatives for women. This project not only improved the living standards of the poorest families, but also brought a change in customary norms. It provides extremely important information for those concerned with rural projects and shows that experts must first learn from rural women before they start teaching them. *(See 248, 279).*

330.   Acharya, Meena, and Lynn Bennett.   "Women and the Subsistence Sector: Economic Participation in Household Decision making in Nepal." World Bank Staff Working Papers No. 526. Washington, D.C.: World Bank, 1983.

Attempts to analyze how socioeconomic and cultural factors affect the extent of labour force participation of rural women in

Nepal. Women's decision making is directly related to their labour force participation. Not only does an increase in women's decision making power have a positive impact on their status, it also raises the well-being of the household and its members. *(See 238, 292).*

331.   Aslanbeigui, Nahid, and Gale Summerfield. "Impact of the Responsibility System on Women in Rural China: An Application of Sen's Theory of Entitlements." World Development 17, no. 3 (March 1989): 343-350.

Evaluates the impact of the responsibility system on women's entitlements in rural China. It argues that the increased wealth of the household does not automatically lead to increased entitlements for all its members. Women may be adversely affected despite an increase in family endowments. *(See 252, 290, 315).*

332.   Breman, Jan. "Between Accumulation and Immiseration: The Partiality of Fieldwork in Rural India." Journal of Peasant Studies 13, no. 1 (October 1985): 5-36.

The author discusses the problems and procedures of his research among the lower classes in rural India and draws general methodological lessons for pursuing fieldwork in the rural areas of any poor country with a polarized class structure. Makes a plea for focusing the research on the lower classes, a population whose voice has remained silent for too long. *(See 244, 257, 271, 620).*

333.   Croll, Elizabeth. Women and Rural Development in China: Production and Reproduction. Geneva: ILO, 1985.

The first part of this book provides a revised version of an earlier monograph written by the author in 1979. The second part discusses the position of women in light of the changes in rural development policy which have taken place in China since 1978. *(See 153, 314).*

334.   Dalsimer, Marlyn, and Laurie Nisonoff. "The Implications of the New Agricultural and One-Child Family Policies for

Rural Chinese Women." Feminist Studies 13, no. 3 (Fall 1987): 583-607.

Examines the implications of recent agricultural and one-child per family policies for rural Chinese women, showing that production and reproduction are closely linked. Makes it clear that these policies benefitted women, but, by and large, had a negative impact on women's health, and social and family status. Suggests alternative policies which minimize risks for rural women. *(See 153, 252, 314, 613)*.

335.   Dixon, Ruth B.   "Mobilizing Women for Rural Employment in South Asia: Issues of Class, Caste, and Patronage." Economic Development and Cultural Change 30, no. 2 (January 1982): 373-390.

Analyses several sources of solidarity and cleavage in agrarian communities in South Asia as a guide to policy makers interested in promoting among women income-generating activities that require co-operation. *(See 244, 246, 257)*.

336.   Duc Nhuân, Nguyên.   "The Contradictions of the Rationalization of Agricultural Space and Work in Vietnam." International Journal of Urban and Regional Research 7, no. 3 (September 1983): 363-79.

Evaluates Vietnamese agricultural planning in the postwar period. This process involved massive mobilization of manual labour, mainly of women, including teenagers and the elderly. In light of the growing inflation, emphasizes the need for the reform of agricultural planning. *(See 631)*.

337.   Epstein, T. Scarlett, and Rosemary A. Watts (eds.). The Endless day: Some Case Material on Asian Rural Women. Oxford: Pergamon Press, 1981.

This book is the product of 'Action Oriented Study on the Role of Asian Women in Rural Development' at the University of Sussex. This collection brings out the complexity of development issues in the Third World countries, and the role of women, in particular rural women, in this process. *(See 257, 335, 614, 620)*.

338.   Gallin, Rita S.   "Women and Work in Rural Taiwan: Building a Contextual Model Linking Employment and Health." Journal of Health and Social Behavior 30, no. 4 (December 1989): 374-85.

Attempts to trace the links between employment and women's health. Emphasizes how global forces and national political economies impinge on culture and how cultural constructs relate to cognitive and bodily responses. *(See 261, 265, 302)*.

339.   Hadi, Abdul Samad. "The Forgotten Contribution: Women and Rural Development in Sabah." SOJOURN 1, no. 2 (August 1986): 199-212.

Analyses the contribution of women relative to men, in the rural economy of Sabah. Women perform a range of activities, but are often regarded as insignificant to the economy. With the rise of wage-work, women are increasingly seen to occupy a subordinate position in the rural economy. *(See 333, 338)*.

340.   Kelkar,   Govind.   "Tractors   against   Women." Development: Seeds of Change. 3 (1985): 18-21.

Assesses the impact of the Green Revolution on rural women in India. Concludes that the Green Revolution precipitated the marginalization of women and helped to increase polarization between the sexes. *(See 3, 176, 578, 620)*.

341.   Lerman, Charles. "Sex-Differential Patterns of Circular Migration: A Case of Semarang, Indonesia." Peasant Studies 10, no. 4 (Summer 1983): 251-269.

This study of circular rural-urban migration is based on interview and official data from Central Java. Suggests that poverty is the main reason behind migration for both men and women. For migrants, including prostitutes, this is an attempt to improve their economic lot. On the whole, women suffer more economic deprivation than men. *(See 298, 317, 629).*

342.   Panigrahi, Sudarsan C., Geeta S. Menon, and Vibha Joshi. "Education of Tribal Women: A Socio-Ecological Perspective." Indian Journal of Social Work 47, no. 4 (January 1987): 417-22.

Focuses on case studies of two villages and discusses the everyday life of tribal women. Brings out the socio-ecological setting which determines the education of women and shows that the existing formal schooling and education have hardly any relevance to the tribal woman and her life. Calls for qualitative changes. *(See 171, 185).*

343.   Pineda, Rosalinda V. "Focus on Filipino Rural Women." Philippine Sociological Review 29, nos 1-4 (January-December 1981): 103-10.

The UN development decade did not affect rural women in the Philippines. Despite their hard work in the rural areas, women still face poverty and their income and position is declining. *(See 130, 237).*

344.   Sharma, Miriam. "Caste, Class, and Gender: Production and Reproduction in North India." Journal of Peasant Studies 12, no. 4 (July 1985): 57-88.

Analyses the effects of the changing gender and class relations in a village in North India and identifies the various social relations that construct women's subordination. Rich and poor women experience oppression in different ways under capitalism. Women have not escaped the sexual hierarchy, but the ideology of patriarchy is being incorporated into capitalist relations. *(See 238, 240, 338).*

345.   Sultana, Monawar. Participation, Empowerment and Variation in Development Projects for Rural Bangladeshi Women. Ph.D. diss., Northeastern University, 1988.

Explores how gender, class and productive activities structure the nature of rural women's participation in projects, and evaluates the impact of program intervention on women's lives in selected NGO development programs. In the absence of programs to maximize poor women's participation in controlling resources, the NGO's contribution to generating income for poor women is minimal. *(See 248, 279, 347, 356).*

346.   Than, Mya. "The Role of Women in Rural Burma: A Case Study." SOJOURN 1, no. 1 (February 1986): 97-108.

This case study of a township in Burma shows the active role of women in production and decision-making. Women play a significant role in all aspects of economic and political life and enjoy relatively equal status. *(See 245).*

347.   White, Sarah C. Arguing With the Crocodile: Gender and Class in Bangladesh. London: Zed Books, 1992.

The author uses first-hand information from her field work in a Bangladeshi village undergoing the Green Revolution to show the centrality of both class and gender in this country. She emphasizes the need to foster people's own perspectives and how they, themselves, interpret their actions. *(See 279, 345, 352).*

348.   Whyte, Robert Orr, and Pauline Whyte. The Women of Rural Asia. Boulder: Westview Press, 1982.

The authors stress the importance of women in the rural development in Asia. The evidence shows that the vital role of women in the family and in the national economy are crucial for development policies. *(See 130, 153, 246).*

3.7 Working for Change

349.   Bakhteari, Quratul Ain. "Building on Traditional Patterns for women Empowerment at Grassroots Level." Development (SID) 4, (1988):55-60.

Describes the achievements of an action program in a village in Pakistan. Through a home-school project women themselves developed programs for the poor, youg and illiterate women. *(See 278, 282, 360)*.

350.   Berninghausen, Jutta, and Birgit Kerstan. Forging New Paths: Feminist Social Methodology and Rural Women in Java. London: Zed Press, 1992.

The author uses the case of Java and stresses the significance of women's self-help organizations. This book documents social change and women's ability to cope with it. *(See 83, 92)*.

351.   Bhatt, Ela. "Toward Empowerment." World Development 17, no. 7 (July 1989): 1059-65.

The author is the founder of the Self-Employed Women's Association, a trade union which has organized a large number of poor women in India. This paper provides a better understanding of the issues that confront workers in the informal sector. It looks for political pressure to increase women's visibility. *(See 141, 226, 430)*.

352.   Dil, Shaheen F. "Women in Bangladesh: Changing Roles and Sociopolitical Realities." Women and Politics 5, no. 1 (Spring 1985): 51-67.

Discusses the sociopolitical and legal position of women in Bangladesh. Women's lives are controlled in multiple ways; however, change is taking place. This article looks at some of these changes in women's position. *(See 347)*.

353.   Dixon, Ruth B.   "Mobilizing Women for Rural Employment in South Asia: Issues of Class, Caste, and Patronage." Economic Development and Cultural Change 30, no. 2 (January 1982): 373-390.

Analyses several sources of solidarity and cleavage in

agrarian communities in South Asia. Provides a guide to policy makers in promoting, among women income-generating activities that require co-operation. *(See 141, 351).*

354.   Griffith, Geoffrey. Village Women Cooperators: An Indian Women's Village Producer Co-operative as Educator and Agent of Social Change. PhD Thesis, University of Sussex, 1987.

Looks in some detail at a particular situation, a voluntary agency called GVA, where women are being given some kind of paid employment. Women are trained as producers and set up in co-operatives so they can manage their own affairs. This thesis provides a critical assessment of the co-operatives and their ability to identify the poor. *(See 149, 222, 367).*

355.   Honig, Emily, and Gail Hershatter. Personal Voices: Chinese Women in the 1980s. Stanford: Stanford University Press, 1988.

This study draws on the periodical press, books on women, and interviews conducted from 1979 to 1986. Each chapter is devoted to an aspect of Chinese women's lives that became a subject of controversy or change in the 1980s. *(See 243, 252, 290, 612).*

356.   Kabeer, Naila. "Organizing Landless Women in Bangladesh." Community Development Journal 20, no. 3 (July 1985): 203-11.

Criticizes development programs for ignoring women or reinforcing their domestic position. Discusses a non-governmental organization's attempt to empower women and enable them to challenge the oppressive social structures. *(See 345, 347).*

357.   Kendall, Laurel, and Mark Peterson (eds.). Korean Women: View from the Inner Room. USA: Laurel Kendall and Mark Peterson, 1983.

This collection of articles presents a variety of female roles which challenge the stereotype of the powerless and dependent Korean woman. It shows that Korean women create for themselves positions of influence which radiate across the narrow ideological and social confines of the Confucian family.

358.   Khan, Nighat Said, Mitha Yameema, Farida Shaheed, and Samina Rehman. "Income Generation for Women: Lessons from the Field in Punjab Province, Pakistan." South Asia Bulletin 9, no. 1 (1989): 26-46.

Discusses the ILO/DANIDA income generating projects for rural women in Pakistan. One was a skill development income generating project, the other an encouragement of date-leaf basketry and the marketing of these products in urban centres. The authors bring out the factors which led to the success of one and the failure of the other project. *(See 276, 361)*.

359.   Lee, Wendy. "Women's Groups in Papua New Guinea: Shedding the Legacy of Drop Scones and Embroidered Pillowcases." Community Development Journal 20, no. 3 (July 1985): 222-36.

Emphasizes the complex reality of the hard life of ordinary Papua New Guinean women. Provides an outline of recent government policies and examines a number of women's groups to see if they are able to offer viable solutions to women's poverty, unemployment, and marginalization in the society. In addition, it discusses the issues and difficulties associated with special projects for women. *(See 295)*.

360.   Mondejar, Ermelina B. "Grassroots Peace Research: Women's Participation in Social Transformation." Alternatives 7, no. 4 (Spring 1982): 533-46.

Describes a successful attempt by the Grassroots Researchers' Training Program in Philippines to enable women to become self-reliant and self-sufficient. This program created a situation where the Grassroots people themselves defined their needs and actively worked to achieve them. *(See 349, 354)*.

361.   Ravindran, Sundari.   "Confronting Gender, Poverty and Powerlessness: An Orientation Programme For and By Rural Change Agents." Community Development Journal 20, no. 3 (July 1985): 213-221.

Attempts are being made by underprivileged women in the Third World countries to define their own priorities and change their conditions of existence. This paper discusses one of those attempts by grassroots women in India. *(See 240, 349, 358)*.

362.   Reddy, G. Narayana.   "Women's Movement: The Indian Scene." Indian Journal of Social Work 46, no. 4 (January 1986): 507-514.

The women's movement in India was overshadowed by Nationalist movements. The post-independence period introduced measures towards women's emancipation, but very little change has been realized. The author believes concrete changes in the status of women are possible with the enforcement of relevant social legislation and the mobilization of women through organizational structure. *(See 145, 150, 363)*.

363.   Rose, Kalima.   Where Women are Leaders: The SEWA Movement in India. London: Zed Books, 1992.

A narrative history of the Self-employed Women's Association (SEWA), a strong union of India's poorest women. This is a living example of a development model which could be used anywhere to save the most vulnerable of women. *(See 145, 150, 362)*.

364.   Rutherford, Andy.   "Strengthening Livestock Rearing Practices of Marginalized Indian Women." Community Development Journal 22, no. 3 (July 1987): 246-50.

Women's groups, in conjunction with a non-governmental group which works in 27 villages in India, have worked and provided solutions for the crisis that was facing the livestock industry. This effort shows that, through organization those marginalized from development programs can become empowered and open new possibilities for themselves. *(See 145, 360, 363).*

365.   Thorbek, Susanne.   "Women and Urbanization."   Acta Sociologica 31, no. 4 (1988): 283-301.

Studies two slums and argues that a new culture is created by the people living in them.   The slum dwellers feel contradictions towards the high culture of their societies.   Women are the central focus of slum culture. *(See 8, 296).*

366.   Vindhya, U., and V. Kalpana.   "Voluntary Organizations and Women's Struggle for Change: Experience with BCT." Indian Journal of Social Work 50, no. 2 (April 1989): 183-97.

Uses an empirical study, conducted on the Bhagavatula Charitable Trust, to examine women's struggle for change from the viewpoint of the contribution of voluntary organizations.   It concludes that the organization of women, solely based on an economic approach, makes little impact on the totality of dependence and injustice. *(See 349, 354).*

367.   Vishwanath, L. S.   "Women's Development through Voluntary Effort: Some Issues and Approaches."   Indian Journal of Social Work 47, no. 3 (October 1986): 293-301.

Emphasizes the stratification of Indian women along the lines of class and caste.   Suggests that NGOs pay attention to this factor and concentrate their efforts on enabling poor women to generate income for themselves. *(See 144, 145, 222, 354).*

Chapter Four

Latin America
and the Caribbean

4.1 Women of Latin America and the Caribbean: An Introduction

368.   Cabestrero, Tefilo. Blood of the Innocent: Victims of the Contras' War in Nicaragua. Maryland: Orbis books, 1985.

This book provides an account of men and women who were the victims of kidnappings, bloody ambushes, rapes, and other kinds of assault by the Contras, and those who survived the slaughter of their families or civilian friends. *(See 378, 387, 580, 647)*.

369.   Ellis, Pat (ed.). Women of the Caribbean. London: Zed Books, 1987.

This collection of essays looks at virtually every aspect of Caribbean women's lives. The authors, all from the region, provide a first-hand account of these women's lives. *(See 373, 389, 392, 394, 411, 443)*.

370.   Harris, Olivia (ed.). Latin American Women. Minority Rights Group Report No. 57. London: Minority Rights Group, 1983.

Provides general information on different aspects of Latin American women's lives. Shows the differences, as well as the similarities, among Latin American women. *(See 6, 25, 393, 403)*.

371.   Holt-Seeland, Inger. Women of Cuba. Westport: Lawrence
        Hill and Co., 1982.

        The author explains in simple terms how the profound
changes that have occurred since the revolution have affected the
lives of the women of Cuba. This book provides a composite
portrait of what life is like for Cuban women. *(See 369, 432,
641)*.

372.   Marshall, Harvey, Letticia Postrada, and Michael Schwartz.
        "Integration into the World System and the Status of
        Women in the Third World." International Journal of
        Contemporary Sociology 25, nos. 3-4 (July-October 1988):
        177-192.

        Uses information from 32 less developed countries in Asia
and South America to show that long and short-term foreign
investment has a negative impact on women's employment in less
developed countries. Integration into the world capitalist system
limits the power and employment prospects of women. Questions
the traditional views of development theory and considers the
differential impact of capitalist investment on men and women.
(See 12, 19, 137).

373.   Massiah, Joycelin. "Women in the Caribbean Project: An
        Overview." Social and Economic Studies 35, no. 2 (June
        1986): 1-29.

        Describes the goals, methodology, and issues related to the
Women in the Caribbean. An important example for developing
frameworks to understand the reality of women. *(See 369)*.

374.   Migration World Magazine 15, nos. 1-2 (1986).

        This issue contains a number of articles which discuss
multiple aspects of migration. It includes articles on domestic
workers in South Africa, Peru, and Sri Lanka. It also discusses
the problems of farm workers in Arizona and garment workers in
New York City. An important discussion of the obstacles that

migrant women--as distinct from migrant men--confront. *(See 8, 10, 196).*

375.   Moser, Caroline O. N. "The Impact of Recession and Structural Adjustment on Women: Ecuador." Development (SID) 1 (1989): 75-83.

Discusses some of the difficulties that face the Ecuadorian economy. Analyses the economic role of women and evaluates the impact of the economic crisis on women. Concludes that women, especially those in the lower income category, carry the burden of economic difficulties. *(See 377).*

376.   Schiefelbein, Ernesto, and Joseph P. Farrell. "Women, Schooling, and Work in Chile: Evidence from a Longitudinal Study." Comparative Education Review 24, no. 2 (June 1980): 160-79.

Women in Chile have more access to high-level occupations than do women in most other societies, and schooling is a more powerful determinant of that access among women than it is among men. This article uses longitudinal data to analyze women's participation in the educational system and their entrance into the labour force. *(See 264, 444, 473).*

377.   Stallings, Barbara, and Robert Kaufman (eds.). Debt and Democracy in Latin America. London: Westview Press, 1989.

This text looks at the impact of the debt crisis on the interaction of socio-political forces in Latin America. The crisis has led to important changes in the perceptions, behaviour and resources of key social groups. *(See 6, 375, 557, 652).*

378.   Thomson, Marilyn. Women of El Salvador: The Price of Freedom. Philadelphia: Institute for the Study of Human Resources, 1986.

The author looks at the impact of the United States war in

Central America on the lives of ordinary peasant and urban women. This book reveals the courage of these women. *(See 281, 368, 387, 638).*

4.2 The Social Construction of Gender

379.   Bunster, Ximena.   "Watch Out for the Little Nazi Man That All of Us Have Inside: The Mobilization and Demobilization of Women in Militarized Chile." Women's Studies International Forum 11, no. 5 (1988): 485-91.

The author analyses the Pinochet regime's discourse on femininity and looks at those women who were active in sustaining that regime. This article shows the division among women and the role of gender ideology in reproducing the status quo. *(See 147, 378).*

380.   Greaves, Thomas C.   "The Woman's Voice in Andean Labour Unions." Urban Anthropology 15, nos. 3-4 (Fall-Winter 1986): 355-76.

Women make critical contributions to the Andean labour movement, but men remain in control of the leadership positions. This article shows how women's contribution is underestimated by the unions. While this article focuses on the Andes, the findings are very relevant for other countries. *(See 639).*

381.   Melhuus, Marit.   "A Shame to Honour--A Shame to Suffer." Ethnos 55, nos. 1-2 (1990): 5-25.

Argues that suffering is the life experience of women. The logic of self-sacrifice works to confirm the identity of women who make the sacrifice. *(See 114, 126, 483).*

382.   Skeen, Patsy, Ligaya Palang Paguio, Bryan E. Robinson, and James E. Deal.   "Mothers Working Outside of the Home: Attitudes of Fathers and Mothers in Three Cultures." Journal of Social Behavior and Personality 3,

no. 4 (1988): 389-98.

Examines the differences in attitudes of American, Brazilian, and Filipino parents regarding mothers working inside and outside the home. *(See 237, 415)*.

383. Van den Hoogen, Lisette. "The Romanization of the Brazilian Church: Women's Participation in a Religious Association in Prados, Minas Gerais." Sociological Analysis 51, no. 2 (Summer 1990): 171-88.

This paper explores women's participation in religious associations and how they feel about their compliance with Catholic behavioural standards. While women have a subordinate position within the church, in certain situations women gain prestige and can exercise influence. The author concludes that the relation between women and the Church can vary in place and time. *(See 48, 469, 477)*.

4.3 Women, State and Development Policies

384. Andreas, Carol. When Women Rebel: The Rise of Popular Feminism in Peru. Westport: L.Hill, 1985.

This book introduces the reader to the recent effects of foreign economic penetration in Peru, both in the city and in the countryside. It discusses the work and political life of the indigenous women of the Andes mountains and demonstrates the negative impacts of the money economy on women. It presents a summary of the outstanding issues facing Peruvian women. *(See 385, 401, 574, 678)*.

385. Bourque, Susan C., and Kay B. Warren. "Multiple Arenas for State Expansion: Class, Ethnicity and Sex in Rural Peru." Ethnic and Racial Studies 3, no. 3 (July 1980): 264-280.

Examines the interplay between state expansion and rural

society's changing responses to ethnic identity, class, and sexual division. The government shows little concern for ethnicity or gender issues. Moreover, the agrarian reform enhanced rural women's dependence on men. Class remains a more complex issue, and state expansion has greatly increased economic stratification. *(See 384, 397, 401, 573, 678)*.

386.   Buvinic, Mayra, Margaret A. Lycette, and William Paul McGreevey. Women and Poverty in the Third World. Baltimore: John Hopkins University Press, 1983.

The essays presented here explore women's contribution to the economy of poor households, and examine the extent of women's poverty. The essays provide information supporting the inclusion of women in development programs. *(See 2, 240)*.

387.   Chomsky, Noam. Turning the Tide: The U.S. and Latin America. Montreal: Black Rose Books, 1987.

This book discusses the aim and impact of U.S. policy in Latin America through the examination of historical record and current events. It helps to understand the broad factors governing U.S. policy in Latin America, and the role of the media and intellectuals in this process. *(See 368, 378, 665, 680)*.

388.   Deere, Carmen Diana. "Rural Women and State Policy: The Latin American Agrarian Reform Experience." World Development 13, no. 9 (September 1985): 1037-51.

Compares thirteen land reforms in Latin America and concludes that, for the most part, land reforms did not have a positive impact on women. Provides suggestions and recommendations to integrate women in the reform policies. *(See 16, 24, 427)*.

389.   Massiah, Joycelin. "Women's Lives and Livelihoods: A View from the Commonwealth Caribbean." World Development 17, no. 7 (July 1989): 965-77.

Despite the favourable economic participation of Caribbean women in the labour market, they face increasing difficulties in light of the current economic crisis. This paper suggests that donor agencies could be more effective if they emphasize plans which enable poor women to earn income. *(See 369, 392).*

390.   Sachs, Carolyn E. "Women, Minorities, and Children as Special Targets of Development in Third World Nations." International Journal of Contemporary Sociology 24, nos. 3-4 (July-October 1987): 113-126.

Development programs have worsened the situation of women, children, and minorities. In the short-term, policies are needed to enhance their access to resources. In the long-term, the process of development itself must be altered to improve the situation of minority groups.

391.   Safa, Helen I. "Urbanization, the Informal Economy and State Policy in Latin America." Urban Anthropology 15, nos. 1-2 (Spring-Summer 1986): 135-63.

Provides a review of recent research on the process of urbanization and industrialization in Latin America and focuses on the relationship between the new international division of labour and the growth of the informal economy. The informal sector can produce cheaply by circumventing labour legislation and by using vulnerable sectors of the labour force, such as women. *(See 8, 178, 200, 568).*

392.   Schuyler, George W., and Henry Veltmeyer (eds.). Rethinking Caribbean Development. Halifax: International Education Centre, 1988.

A collection of papers by key figures in Caribbean studies which draws attention to the region's problems. It argues that it is time to rethink development theories and policies and learn from the past mistakes. This requires a realistic plan for the future of the region, one which has meaning for the people. *(See 369, 389, 394, 406).*

393.   Tavera, Helena Paez de. "Les effets de la crise sur les
       femmes." in Terrence McGrath (ed.). The Crisis in Latin
       America/La Crise en Amérique Latine. Ottawa: University
       of Ottawa Press, 1987.

Looks at the impact of the crisis in Latin America on
women and argues that structural changes in the global economy
are bringing hardship to women. The answer lies in collective
action by women themselves. *(See 6, 25, 370).*

394.   Thomas, Clive Y. The Poor and the Powerless: Economic
       Policy and Change in the Caribbean. New York: Monthly
       Review Press, 1988.

This book critically evaluates development policies in the
Caribbean from the perspective of the majority of the people. The
survey presented here covers the plantation system and slavery of
the past to the activities of multinational corporations of the present
time. It draws from specific causes, and it argues that we need a
development for and by the ordinary people. *(See 369, 392, 443).*

395.   Tiano, Susan. "Export Processing, Women's Work, and
       the Employment Problem in Developing Countries: The
       Case of the Maquiladora Program in Northern Mexico."
       Western Sociological Review 15, no. 1 (1986): 53-78.

This article uses the case of Mexico and shows the impact
of large-scale movement of capital on employment practices in the
Third World countries. Unemployment persists despite considerable
investment in export-processing industrialization. *(See 1, 12, 19,
266, 397, 418).*

396.   Wiarda, Ieda Siqueira, and Judith Frye Helzner. "Women,
       Population, and International Development in Latin
       America: A 1984 Assessment." Managing International
       Development MID. 1, no. 5 (September-October 1984):
       84-106.

Looks back at women's exclusion from population and

development policy and action. Until recently, women have been excluded from policy considerations and programs. Development theories and policies have evolved from a Western ethnocentric view which treated countries as homogeneous wholes. Discusses some of the changes which are taking place in old policies and theories and the importance of such changes. *(See 13, 17, 159)*.

4.4 Work and Family

397.   Beneria, L., and M. Roldan. The Cross Roads of Class and Gender: International Homework, Subcontracting and Household Dynamics in Mexico City. Chicago: University of Chicago Press, 1987.

The global restructuring of the economy has increased the demand for flexible workers. Homework provides such flexibility, and also enables workers to fight with unemployment and raise the family budget. Women are a major source of the cheap labour engaged in domestic industry. This book shows vividly the inter-relationship between gender and class in the reproduction of the global economy. *(See 26, 271, 395, 412)*.

398.   Browner, C. H. "Gender Roles and Social Change: A Mexican Case Study." Ethnology 25, no. 2 (April 1986): 89-106.

Women's response to change is affected by both internal and external factors in their communities and by the nature of mother-child relations. Interest and opportunity must be present for women to support social change. *(See 2, 12, 18)*.

399.   Browner, C. H. "Women, Household and Health in Latin America." Social Science and Medicine 28, no. 5 (1989): 461-73.

Using the household as a unit of analysis can be a powerful lens through which to view the uneven impact of capitalism on health in Latin America. In doing so, this paper discusses women's health and their role as health providers. The articulation between women's productive and reproductive roles is having profound effects on their health and that of their children. *(See 2, 113).*

400.   Bunster, Ximena, and Elsa M. Chaney.   Sellers and Servants: Working Women in Lima, Peru.   New York: Prager, 1985.

The authors use both qualitative and quantitative methods to study poor women in the labour force in Peru. Their focus is on domestic service, street selling and market vending. They document women's work and family life, and how these women struggle to improve their conditions. *(See 198, 299, 384, 385, 433).*

401.   Mallon, Florencia E.   "Patriarchy in the Transition to Capitalism: Central Peru, 1830-1950."   Feminist Studies 13, no. 2 (Summer 1987): 379-407.

Alters the debate on the persistence of household production in the Third World countries and argues that class analysis by itself is not sufficient. Only the careful combination of class and gender can enable us to understand the reality of Latin America. *(See 19, 384, 385).*

402.   Nash, June.   "The Mobilization of Women in the Bolivian Debt Crisis."   Barbara A. Gutek, Ann H. Stromberg, Laurie Linwood (eds.).   Women and Work: An Annual Review Vol.3.   Newbury Park: Sage Publications Inc., 1988.

The debt crisis is deepening in Latin America. In Bolivia, more than ever before, women are forced to work in the informal sector of the economy to help their families survive. The collapse of the productive base of the country has moved the class struggle to a struggle based on life and bread. In this process, the changing role of women plays a major part. *(See 6, 25, 26, 652).*

403.   Nash, June.   "Latin American Women in the World
        Capitalist Crisis." Gender and Society 4, no. 3 (September
        1990): 338-353.

        The author uses a number of cases from Latin America to
demonstrate the centrality of women's work. This article ensures
that domestic production is becoming the central arena for
developing consciousness and revolutionary change in the present
crisis of capitalism. *(See 12, 19, 370, 397, 415, 445, 646, 655).*

404.   Phillips, Lynne.   "Gender Dynamics and Rural Household
        Strategies." Canadian Review of Sociology and
        Anthropology 26, no. 2 (May 1989): 294-310.

        Looks at gender dynamics within rural households in
Ecuador and helps to expand our understanding of the extent to
which women play a role in maintaining and transforming family
relations. *(See 2, 60, 406).*

405.   Powell, Dorian.   "The Role of Women in the Caribbean."
        Social and Economic Studies 33, no. 2 (June 1984): 97-
        122.

        This paper discusses the multiple roles of women in
Caribbean society. Women have been active in both the private
and the public spheres. However, there has been an overemphasis
on women's domestic role.   Without supporting women's
involvement in various levels of public life, their meaningful
integration into development programs is not possible. *(See 369,
373, 392).*

406.   Radcliffe, Sarah A.   "Between Hearth and Labor Market:
        The Recruitment of Peasant Women in the Andes."
        International Migration Review 24, no. 2 (Summer 1990):
        229-49.

        Distinguishes various agents for the recruitment of Andean
women into the extra-local labour force. Recruitment of peasants
into external labour markets and their migration from the

community is determined by the relationship between gender, family position, and the structure of the labour market. *(See 6, 78, 404, 639)*.

407.   Winter, Mary, Earl W. Morris, and Arthur D. Murphy. "Planning and Implementation in the Informal Sector: Evidence from Oaxaca, Mexico." City and Society 4, no. 2 (December 1990): 131-43.

This study examines planning strategies among women in the informal sector in a city in Mexico. The research is carried out at a micro-level, with ethnographic data from individual households on the economics of their particular informal sector activity. *(See 178, 296)*.

408.   Wyer, June. "Child Labour in Brazilian Agriculture." Critique of Anthropology 6, no. 2 (Summer 1986): 63-80.

This paper suggests that in the Brazilian Amazon the use to which children's work is put is determined, to a large extent, by the economic position and function assumed by women in the household. *(See 241, 286)*.

4.5 Women's Experience of Wage-Work

409.   Babb, Florence E.   "Women's Work: Engendering Economic Anthropology." Urban Anthropology 19, no. 3 (Fall 1990): 277-302.

Focuses on the informal economy in the Peruvian Andes and shows the centrality of gender.   Argues that studies are incomplete when they disregard gender. *(See 413, 415, 678)*.

410.   Brockmann, C. Thomas. "Women and Development in Northern Belize." Journal of Developing Areas 19, no. 4 (July 1985): 501-513.

Criticizes the Western model of economic development and

shows that the intensification of market relations in Belize, a newly independent country in the Caribbean, has reinforced the existing inequalities. While men's position is enhanced, women have become weaker and more dependent on men. As well, subsistence production is no longer viable, and for the poor, increased market involvement has not brought prosperity. *(See 2, 12)*.

411.   Carty, Linda. "Women and Labour Force Participation in the Caribbean." Fireweed 24 (Winter 1987): 39-53.

Addresses gender inequality in the Caribbean labour force in the global context of capitalist accumulation. Using the Caribbean case as an example, the author shows clearly the connection between women's subordination in the labour force and the accumulation of capital in dependent social formations. *(See 369, 392)*.

412.   Dixon, Marlene, Elizabeth Martínez, Ed McCaughan, and Susanne Jonas. "Chicanos and Mexicanos within a Transnational Working Class: Theoretical Perspectives." Review 7, no. 1 (Summer 1983): 109-50.

Presents an analysis of Chicanos and Mexicanos as a transnational working class, and within that, the role and status of women. It emphasizes the transnational character of capital in the modern capitalist world economy, unfettered by the limitations of nationalism or the legal fictions of national boundaries. *(See 7, 12, 397, 425)*.

413.   Draper, Elaine. "Women's Work and Development in Latin America." Studies in Comparative International Development 20, no. 1 (Spring 1985): 3-30.

Discusses the limitations of the modernization theory and examines the impact of capitalist development on women's work. Focuses on the analysis of women's work in Latin America and raises issues which highlight the need to sharpen conceptual tools in the study of development. *(See 18, 22, 23, 423)*.

414.   Garcia de Fanelli, Ana María. "The Role of Women in
        Public Enterprises: The Case of Argentina." Public
        Enterprise 10, nos. 3-4 (September-December 1990): 319-
        36.

The author focuses on Argentina and looks at women's
position in the labour market. Not only are women concentrated
in certain types of occupations, they are absent in the upper level
of the occupational hierarchy and decision making. *(See 370, 403,
409).*

415.   Hirata, Helena, and John Humphrey. "Crise economique
        et emploi des femmes. Une Etude de cas dans l'industrie
        bresilienne." Sociologie du Travail 26, no. 3 (July-
        September 1984): 278-89.

Uses theories of segmented labour market and the reserve
army of labour to discuss women's position in Brazilian industry.
Argues that crisis and depression have different impacts on men
and women. *(See 6, 403, 413).*

416.   Humphrey, John. "The Growth of Female Employment in
        Brazilian Manufacturing Industry in the 1970s." Journal of
        Development Studies 20, no. 4 (July 1984): 224-47.

Looks at Brazil between 1970 and 1980 and questions the
pessimistic prediction of some versions of the dependency theory
that dependent industrial development marginalizes women in the
industrial labour force. Provides a detailed pattern of increasing
female employment in different industries. *(See 403, 409, 416).*

417.   Humphrey, J. Gender and Work in the Third World:
        Sexual Division in Brazilian Industry. London: Tavistock
        Publication, 1987.

The author questions that women workers are marginalized,
confined to certain types of industries or are part of a 'reserve
army of labour'. However, it is argued that there are barriers
which prevent women from entering into top level positions. This

book provides rich information on the Brazilian labour market. *(See 113, 114, 416).*

418.   Kelly, Deirdre. "St. Lucia's Female Electronics Factory Workers: Key Components in an Export-Oriented Industrialization Strategy." World Development 14, no. 7 (July 1986): 823-838.

This essay is based on a series of in-depth interviews with female electronic production workers in St. Lucia and criticizes export-oriented industrialization for its negative impact on women. It concludes that a strategy for development based solely, or largely on the production of labour-intensive goods for export to industrialized countries is unadvisable. *(See 1, 19, 266, 395, 420, 422, 425).*

419.   Lautier, Bruno. "Wage Relationship, Informal Sector and Employment Policy in South America." Journal of Development Studies 26, no.2 (January 1990): 278-298.

Stresses the importance of the informal sector in the economy of Third World countries and addresses the heterogeneity of this particular type of economic organization. Calls for a new economic policy which avoids to formalize this sector. *(See 8, 178, 296).*

420.   Peña, Devon, and Gilbert Cardenas.   "The Division of Labor in Microelectronics: A Comparative Analysis of France, Mexico, and the United States." Studies in Comparative International Development 23, no. 2 (Summer 1988): 89-112.

Focuses on the microelectronic industry and provides a comparative analysis of the division of labour. The three case studies reveal a universal gender-based division of labour where women have a subordinate position. Emphasises the fact that women have a subordinate position in the sexual division of labour, both in developed and developing countries. *(See 266, 311, 418).*

421.   Reddock, Rhoda.   "Women and Garment Production in
       Trinidad and Tobago 1900-1960."   Social and Economic
       Studies 39, no. 1 (March 1990): 89-125.

This study focuses on the garment and textile industry in
Trinidad and Tobago between 1900 and 1960.   This historical
discussion traces the changing forms of women's participation in
the industrial sector within the context of the overall economy.   As
well, it shows the transformation of the social relations of
production in the garment industry from petty commodity to large-
scale mass production.

422.   Ríos, Palmira N.   "Export-Oriented Industrialization and
       the Demand for Female Labor: Puerto Rican Women in the
       Manufacturing Sector, 1952-1980."   Gender and Society 4,
       no. 3 (September 1990): 321-337.

Export-oriented development programs in Puerto Rico
brought a large number of women into the manufacturing sector.
This article examines gender-segregated development patterns
which are shaped by economic, political, social, and cultural
constraints.   The apparent contradiction between government
policies and the employment practices of the manufacturing sector
is due to the restructuring of the global economy.   *(See 19, 266,
395, 418, 420).*

423.   Rosa, Del, and Judy Labarca.   "The Economic Crisis and
       the Criminalization of Latin American Women."   Social
       Justice 17, no. 2 (Summer 1990): 40-53.

The burgeoning drug trade and increasing unemployment
have changed the picture of criminality in Latin America.   Women
have found a new source of employment and are subject to a
severe criminalization process.   Provides new conceptual
frameworks to analyze the problem of drug-related criminalization.
(See 6, 403, 413).

424.   Terrell, Katherine.   "An Analysis of the Wage Structure in
       Guatemala City."   Journal of Developing Areas 23, no. 3

(April 1989): 405-424.

This study of workers in Guatemala City analyses the determinants of workers' income by individual characteristics, occupation, and industry. Focuses on gender-related discrimination and shows that different forces are at work in determining wage-levels in the formal and informal sectors. *(See 370, 413, 429).*

425.   Tiano, Susan.   "Maquiladoras, Women's Work, and Unemployment in Northern Mexico."   Aztlan 15, no. 2 (Fall 1984): 341-78.

The author argues that the role of the Border Industrialization Program in Northern Mexico can only be understood in relation to the social and economic arrangements. The composition of the Maquiladora labour force, and the impact of the program on workers and their families, reflect these social realities. *(See 7, 12, 397, 412, 418).*

4.6 Working in the Rural Areas

426.   Burbach, Roger, and Patricia Flynn. Agribusiness in the Americas. New York: Monthly Review Press and North American Congress on Latin America, 1980.

The food crisis has receded from the headlines, but this book shows that hunger and malnutrition are the brutal reality for a large portion of humanity. This book analyzes the workings and impact of agribusiness on agricultural production and hunger. In both the United States and the Third World, the growing dominance of agribusiness typically means that vast numbers of small farmers are continually being deprived of their means of production. *(See 16, 24).*

427.   Deere, Carmen Diana, and Magdalena León de Leal. "Peasant Production, Proletarianization, and the Sexual Division of Labor in the Andes." Signs 7, no. 2 (Winter 1981): 338-360.

Shows that material conditions are the key in explaining the sexual division of labour in production. To understand women's subordination, we need to look at the sexual division of labour between production and reproduction. *(See 388).*

428.   Ellis, Pat. "Equipping Women for Fuller Participation in the Process of Rural Development." Community Development Journal 22, no. 2 (April 1987): 135-40.

Discusses a pilot project which was implemented in 1980 in a village in the British West Indies in order to increase rural women's participation in the development process of this community. A good example of a participatory approach to development. *(See 4, 11, 60).*

429.   Herbenar Bossen, L. The Redivision of Labor: Women and Economic Choice in Four Guatemalan communities. Albany: State University of New York, 1984.

This study combines qualitative and quantitative data and looks at the sexual division of labour among the peasantry, the plantation workers, the middle class and the poor in the urban areas. It shows the importance of class and regional differences and stresses the importance of economic changes on women's status. *(See 370, 424).*

430.   Jarrett, Stephen. "A Revolving Fund to Provide the Capital for Self-Help: Rural Women's Small Production Units in Honduras." Assignment Children 49-50 (Spring 1980): 141-53.

This case study shows that in order to increase the impact of rural development projects in poor areas, the economic issues have to be addressed first. By providing revolving capital to women for small production units, rapid delivery of services was possible. These projects provided women with supplementary income as well as management skills. *(See 141, 351).*

431.   Lastarría-Cornhiel, Susana.   "Female Farmers and

Agricultural Production in El Salvador." Development and Change 19, no. 4 (October 1988): 585-615.

Very few studies on women in rural households have examined their agricultural output and productivity vis-a-vis men. This study uses data collected in El Salvador in 1984 to fill this gap. It focuses on access to resources, agricultural production and other income generating activities of rural households, comparing male and female farmers. *(See 378).*

432.   Stubbs, Jean. "Gender Issues in Contemporary Cuban Tobacco Farming." World Development 15, no. 1 (January 1987): 41-65.

Focuses on tobacco farming, and discusses the sexual division of labour and the changing relations of production in the family unit. Particular attention is paid to the position of women in the co-operative farming units. *(See 153, 371).*

433.   Vergolino, Tercina Barbosa. Maids and Mistresses in Recife (Brazil): An Analysis of Linkages between the Formal and Informal Economy. Ph.D. Thesis. Urbana: University of Illinois at Urbana-Champaign, 1989.

This study focuses on a special category of workers in the informal sector, namely domestic servants. Domestic service absorbs a significant number of workers, mainly female, in Brazil. The author discusses the importance of domestic service for the process of development in Brazil. *(See 198, 400).*

434.   Wilson, Fiona. "Women and Agricultural Change in Latin America: Some Concepts Guiding Research." World Development 13, no. 9 (September 1985): 1017-35.

Reviews the literature on the impact of commercialization and capitalism on the lives of rural women in Latin America, drawing attention to the conceptual and political differences among the commentators. As well, it emphasizes the similarities shared by these studies. *(See 413, 426).*

435.   Young, Kate.   "Changing Economic Roles of Women in
        Two Rural Mexican Communities." Sociologia Ruralis 18,
        nos. 2-3 (1978): 197-216.

        The author argues that the profound changes in the Mexican
economy had negative impact on women, and uses the research on
two rural communities to discuss the national and local economic
development, the disintegration of subsistence production and the
development of capitalist production. In this process, women lost
their control and autonomy and acquired a more subordinate
position. What is needed is a policy which recognizes women's
contributions and develops plans to support and enhance their
position. *(See 370, 403).*

4.7 Working for Change

436.   Andreas,   Carol.   "People's   Kitchens   and   Radical
        Organizing in Lima, Peru." Monthly Review 41, no. 6
        (November 1989): 12-21.

        A growing number of people's kitchens were established in
Peru to respond to the acute issues of survival and reproduction.
Women play an important role in the administration of these
people's kitchens and have acquired a new source of political
power. This discussion shows that people's kitchens can be
adopted as a means to empower poor people. *(See 367, 384, 385).*

437.   Angel, Adriana, and Fiona Macintosh. The Tiger's Milk:
        Women of Nicaragua. London: Virago Press, 1987.

        The authors provide a powerful illustration of the voices of
Nicaraguan women, young and old, describing the moving details
of their everyday lives. Women are challenging traditional norms
and are helping to shape the new country. *(See 370).*

438.   Barndt, Deborah.   Education and Social Change: A
        Photographic Study of Peru. New York: Kendall/Hunt
        Publishing Company, 1980.

Explores the dynamics of the 'conscientization' process introduced by Freire and adopts a critical approach to education in Peru. Rather than beginning with the theory, the author begins with the context, exploring from the ground up some notions that emerged within this process. *(See 384, 385, 436, 662).*

439. Barrios de Chungara, Domitila with Moema Viezzer. Let Me Speak: Testimony of Domitila, a Woman of the Bolivian Mines. (Translated by Victoria Ortiz). New York: Monthly Review Press, 1978.

A moving account of the life of a working woman who became a leader of a 'Housewives Committee' dedicated to improving miners' and peasants' conditions. This is a rich and insightful oral history. *(See 54, 76, 673).*

440. Campfens, Hubert. "Issues in Organizing Impoverished Women in Latin America." Social Development Issues 13, no. 1 (Fall 1990): 20-43.

The economic condition of women has declined despite the attempts made during the UN decade for development. Women have been relegated to an inferior status. This study shows how popular women's organizations can be of rich potential for development. *(See 54, 439, 645).*

441. Crandon, Libbet, and Bonnie Shepard. Women, Enterprise, and Development. Chestnut Hill: Pathfinder Fund, 1984.

This study is about five women's income-generating projects: metal working in Brazil; an ice cream factory in Costa Rica; poultry production in Honduras; a bakery in Honduras; and crafts production in Jamaica. All five projects have been successful and have been integrated into the formal economy. *(See 2, 29, 64).*

442. Hahner, June E. Emancipating the Female Sex: The Struggle for Women's Rights in Brazil, 1850-1940.

Durham: Duke University Press, 1990.

This book looks at Brazilian women's fight for emancipation, from its earliest manifestations in the 19th century to the successful achievement of the suffrage campaign in the 1930s. The author interviews surviving Brazilian suffragists. *(See 78, 370)*.

443.   Haniff, Nesha. Blaze a Fire: Significant Contributions of Caribbean Women. Toronto: Sister Vision, 1988.

The author brings together a profile of 28 Caribbean women and illustrates the changing attitudes and roles of women in the Caribbean--their living and working conditions and their struggles individually and collectively. *(See 369, 373, 394)*.

444.   Kirkwood, Julieta.   "Women and Politics in Chile." International Social Science Journal 35, no. 4 (1983): 625-37.

The emergence of women's awareness has profound social, cultural, and historical origins; however, it has been ignored. This study provides a historical account of feminist activities in Chile and shows that it is only since 1978 that there has been an emphasis on feminist issues. *(See 370, 376)*.

445.   Nash, June, Helen Safa and contributors. Women and Change in Latin America. Mass.: Bergin and Garvey Publishers, 1985.

An insightful account of women's roles in development and change in Latin America. It addresses complex issues and with original research, provides a new model for viewing complex problems in studying women. *(See 370, 403, 666)*.

446.   Neuhouser, Kevin.   "Sources of Women's Power and Status among the Urban Poor in Contemporary Brazil." Signs 14, no. 3 (Spring 1989): 685-702.

Uses ethnographic and qualitative data to talk about resources available to poor urban women in Brazil. Shows that the impact of capitalist development on women is not homogeneous. Lower-class women in the cities have more chance for employment than men. Working in the cities equips women with certain resources that enable them to experience mobility, develop contacts, and improve their economic position. *(See 361, 439)*.

447.   Smith-Ayala, Emilie. The Granddaughter of Ixmucane: Guatemalan Women Speak (translated as told to Emilie Smith-Ayala). Toronto: Women's Press, 1991.

This book provides a rich account of women's lives in Guatemala, as told by the women themselves. It is an important contribution, and shows that despite the military, there is a vast tapestry of hope. *(See 54, 76, 651, 672, 675)*.

448.   Young, Gay. "Women, Development, and Human Rights: Issues in Integrated Transnational Production." Journal of Applied Behavioral Science 20, no. 4 (November 1984): 383-401.

Looks at the employment of women in large multinational corporations in Mexico's Border Industrialization Program to show that women are participants in development. This type of integration into economic development does not enable women to enhance self-respect and become active participants in shaping their communities. *(See 397, 403, 436)*.

449.   Zeidenstein, Sondra. "A Regional Approach to Women's Needs: The Women and Development Unit in the Caribbean." Assignment Children 49-50 (Spring 1980): 155-71.

The Women and Development Unit, WAND, was created to respond to the expressed needs of women in the Caribbean countries. This paper discusses the plans, activities, and achievements of this organization. *(See 369, 373)*.

Chapter Five

The Middle East

5.1 Women of the Middle East: An Introduction

450. Alsuwaigh, Siham A. "Women in Transition: The Case of
      Saudi Arabia." Journal of Comparative Family Studies 20,
      no. 1 (Spring 1989): 67-78.

      The socio-economic changes in Saudi Arabia together with
urbanization and advances in education have had a major impact on
the lives of women. The author, a female Saudi, discusses some
of these changes in this article. *(See 465, 502, 504, 524).*

451. Ata, A. W. "Impact of Westernization and Other Factors
      on the Changing Status of Moslem Women." Eastern
      Anthropologist 37, no. 2 (1984): 95-126.

      This paper examines the influence of the West on the
position of Moslem women against the background of the Middle
East's traditional social pattern. It shows the ambivalent attitudes
that Middle Eastern people have towards the West. *(See 499, 518,
530, 580, 686).*

452. Austrin, Nabila Jaber. Modernization, Legal Reforms and
      the Place of Women in Muslim Developing Countries.
      Ph.D. Thesis. Southern Illinois University, 1987.

      This thesis is a critical evaluation of the status of women in

Muslim developing countries in the context of both modernization and legal reforms. Uses data from fifteen countries and concludes that legal secularization in the domestic sphere is a necessary condition for women's advancement in the public sphere. *(See 499, 510, 517)*.

453.   Burke III, Edmund (ed.).   Struggle and Survival in the Modern Middle East. London: I.B. Tauris, 1993.

This book attempts to write the history of the Middle East from the point of view of ordinary people. It assembles biographies of 24 ordinary people, from various walks of life, and provides an account of Middle Eastern history. It provides much information on pre-colonial, colonial and contemporary Middle East. *(See 2, 570)*.

454.   Calderini, Simonetta.   A Decade of Middle East Research (at the School of Oriental and African Studies, University of London). London: Centre for Near and Middle Eastern Studies, 1991.

This bibliography provides an overview of Middle Eastern related research at the School of Oriental and African Studies. *(See 93, 457, 466)*.

455.   Dearden, Ann (ed.).   Arab Women.   Minority Rights Group Report No. 27, Revised 1983 Edition. London: Minority Rights Group, 1983.

Provides general information about different aspects of Arab women's lives. Brings out the differences in the social and political lives of women in various countries. *(See 93, 454, 461, 462, 521)*.

456.   Early, Evelyn A.   Baladi Women of Cairo: Playing With an Egg and a Stone. Boulder: Lynne Rienner Publishers, 1992.

The author explores Baladi women's identity by recording

their everyday discourse and how they handle such issues as housing, work, marriage, and religion. This book provides much information on Baladi women's everyday life. *(See 2)*.

457.   Gadant, Monique (ed.).   Women of the Mediterranean. London: Zed Books, 1986.

This collection addresses various issues which face women in the Mediterranean. The authors show the diversity among Mediterranean women and stress the common problems and experiences of women who live in this area. *(See 454, 475, 537)*.

458.   Gran, Judith.   "Impact of the World Market on Egyptian Women."   MERIP Reports No. 58 (June 1977): 3-7.

Provides a class analysis of women's position in Egypt. The status and ideology of women varies by their class position. With the intensification of the economic crisis, it is likely that women will be pressed to go "back-to-the-home." It is also possible that the economic crisis, and a need for double income in the family, will force women to work outside the house. *(See 503, 509, 513, 517)*.

459.   Harlow, Barbara.   "Narrative in Prison: Stories from the Palestinian Intifada."   Modern Fiction Studies 35, no. 1 (Spring 1989): 29-46.

The author reviews the expanding literature on the lives of Palestinian women living under Israeli occupation. Discusses the importance of the essay "Intifada or Revolution" in recent events in the Occupied Territories. Palestinian women's stories as well as the Intifada are yielding to narrating history and reading narrative. *(See 463, 525, 549, 683)*.

460.   Hijab, Nadia.   Women Power: The Arab Debate on Women at Work. Cambridge: Cambridge University Press, 1988.

This book is about the Arab World today--its society,

economy, and politics--as seen through an examination of the debate on Arab women at work. The author paints a picture drawn from individual stories, as well as from national development programs, to explain why the process of social change has been slow. *(See 455, 527).*

461.   Hourani, Albert, Philip Khoury, and Mary Wilson. The Modern Middle East: A Reader. London: I.B. Tauris, 1992.

This collection presents key writings on the modern history of the Middle East by some of the most distinguished scholars in this area. This book serves as a general introduction and familiarizes its readers with the central issues in the Middle East. *(See 455).*

462.   Keddie, Nikki R., and Beth Baron. (eds.). Women in Middle East History. New Haven: Yale University Press, 1991.

This rich collection deals with the major aspects of the Middle Eastern women's history. It uses a historical approach and suggests that gender boundaries in the Middle East have been neither fixed nor immutable. *(See 93, 454, 455).*

463.   Nassrallah, Emily. A House Not Her Own: Stories from Beirut. Ragweed Press and Gynery books, 1992.

In this collection of stories an award-winning Lebanese author writes about war and its devastating impact on people. The author provides a fascinating account of women's day-to-day lives in the bombed-out shell of Beirut. *(See 459, 525, 691, 692).*

464.   Sherif, Mostafa Hashem. "What is Hijab?" The Muslim World LXXVII, nos. 3-4 (July-October 1987): 151-63.

Contemporary Islamists have looked at Hijab (the covering of women's hair) as a matter of necessity. This article argues that Hijab has meant different things for different people. One must view dress as a coded message that reflects political and ideological choices. It is concluded that the overwhelming majority of the interpretations of Hijab can neither be traced back to the Prophet nor to his contemporaries. *(See 467, 468, 485, 681).*

465. Soffan, Linda Usra. The Women of United Arab Emirates. London: Croom Helm, 1980.

This book looks at the factors which have influenced and continue to affect the position held by women in (UAE) today. It pays particular attention to the impact of Islamic Law. *(See 450, 528).*

466. UNESCO, Social Science Research and Women in the Arab world. Paris: UNESCO, 1984.

This book presents studies prepared for a UNESCO meeting on 'Multidisciplinary Research on Women in the Arab World' (Tunis 1982). Information gathered from Algeria, Egypt, Iraq, Libya, Morocco, Saudi Arabia, Tunisia and Sudan is used to describe the situation of women and research on women in these countries. *(See 454).*

467. Waines, David. "Through a Veil Darkly: The Study of Women in Muslim Societies. A Review Article." Comparative Studies in Society and History 24, no. 4 (October 1982): 642-59.

Provides a survey of literature on women in Middle Eastern society. Adds to the recent work which offers the possibility of revising some of the traditional stereotypes not only of Muslim women, but also of Muslim culture in a broader sense. *(See 464, 476, 485).*

468. Yeganeh, Nahid, and Nikki R. Keddie. "Sexuality and Shi'i Social Protest in Iran" in Cole, Juan R. I., and Nikki R. Keddie, ed. Shi'ism and Social Protest. New Haven: Yale University Press, 1986.

Islamic movements demonstrate that the socio-political context is important in determining the form and content of sexuality. This study questions any universal concept of sexuality in Islam. *(See 270, 464, 469, 470, 471, 688).*

5.2 The Social Construction of Gender

469.   Bauer, Janet L. "Sexuality and the Moral 'Construction' of Women in an Islamic Society." Anthropological Quarterly 58, no. 3 (July 1985): 120-29.

This study uses the case of Iran to discuss the importance of the social context in the construction of gender and morality. It shows that sexuality and sexual behaviour are bases for the moral construction of women, and that women themselves make moral judgements regarding behavioural obligations to others. *(See 165, 270, 471, 688).*

470.   El Saadawi, Nawal. The Hidden Face of Eve: Women in the Arab World. Boston: Beacon Press, 1982.

The author--Egypt's former Director of Public Health, a doctor, novelist and feminist--paints a vivid picture of what it means to grow up female in an Islamic society. A very helpful introduction to anyone interested in understanding the position of Arab women. *(See 93, 464, 467).*

471.   Elias, Jamal J.   "Female and Feminine in Islamic Mysticism." The Muslim World LXXVIII, nos. 3-4 (July-October 1988): 209-224.

Looks at feminine mysticism and its role in Sufism. It shows that idealized woman had played a major role in the development of Sufi philosophy. Women are essential in this belief system. Women are never equal to men and on a scale of perfection they are above the male and below the male. *(See 165, 469, 470, 506, 688).*

472.   Friedl, Erika. "Islam and Tribal Women in a Village in Iran." in Nancy A. Falk and Rita M. Gross (eds.). Unspoken Worlds: Women's Religious Lives in Non-Western Cultures. San Francisco: Harper & Row, 1980.

Discusses the way in which religious knowledge is learned and transmitted, the role women play in religious rituals, the criteria used to distinguish morally good and bad women and men, and the relationship between women's self-image and their world views within one of the tribal villages in Iran. *(See 474, 493, 693)*.

473.   Ghorayshi, Parvin. "Gender Disparity in Education: A Challenge for Development. International Journal of Contemporary Sociology 30, no.2, 1993.

This article underlines the complex factors that negatively affect women's access to education. The social and political construction of gender have adverse impact on women's participation in the educational ladder. *(See 264, 376, 512)*.

474.   Hegland, Mary Elaine. "'Traditional' Iranian Women: How They Cope." The Middle East Journal 36, no. 4 (Autumn 1982): 483-501.

This article discusses the conditions and attitudes of traditional Iranian women. These women's freedom is contained within the boundaries set by men and other traditional authorities. After the Revolution, force and fear were added to the economic and social dependence of traditional women.

475.   Izos, Peter, and Evthymios Paptaxiarchis (eds.). Contested Identities: Gender and Kinship in Modern Greece. New Jersey: Princeton University Press, 1991.

This publication provides a comprehensive view of what it means to be a Greek man or woman, married or unmarried and having kinship ties. It looks at the process through which sexual identity is established and shows the complexity of the issues. *(See*

33, 47).

476.   Journal of South Asian and Middle Eastern Studies Vol. 4,
       no. 2 (Winter 1980).

There are three articles in the Winter issue of this journal
which look at the role of Islam in determining women's position.
The impact of religion on women's lives is strong and contributes
to the reproduction of women's subordinate position. *(See 464,
467, 468).*

477.   Kaufman, Debra Renee.   Rachel's Daughters: Newly
       Orthodox Jewish Women. London: Rutgers University
       Press, 1991.

This book puts together the stories of 150 newly orthodox
Jewish women: young women who were recruited by the Western
Wall during their trips to Israel. The author tries to explain why
the women were attracted to a tradition in which the laws and
customs are patriarchal. *(See 63, 544).*

478.   Mabro, Judy.   Veiled Half-Truths: Western Travellers'
       Perceptions of Middle Eastern Women.   London: I.B.
       Tauris and Co. Ltd., 1991.

A shocking anthology of European travel writings about
Oriental women. Travellers wrote about harem, veil, and sexuality
obsessively, producing images of women as unreal and
contradictory. *(See 72, 75, 99, 492).*

479.   Malek, Alloula.   The Colonial Harem.   Translated by
       Myrna Godzich and Wlad Godzich; Introduced by Barbara
       Harlow.   Minneapolis: University of Minnesota Press,
       1986.

The author has collected, arranged and annotated the picture
postcards of Algerian women produced and sent by the French in
Algeria during the first three decades of this century. It presents
a literary-historical response to the challenges of French

colonialism which continues to influence present-day Algeria. *(See 72, 75).*

480.   Marcous, Julie. <u>A World of Difference: Islam and Gender Hierarchy in Turkey</u>. London: Zed Press, 1992.

The author examines the hierarchical aspects of Islamic religion and its impact on women. She provides a feminist critique of the politics of knowledge and illustrates how sexuality has played a crucial role in the subordination of East to West. *(See 72, 75, 275).*

481.   Mernissi, Fatima. "Muslim Women and Fundamentalism." <u>Middle East Report</u>. (July-August 1988): 8-11, 50.

Attempts to explain how women fit in the present conflicting forces which characterize the Muslim world. Discusses fundamental changes in sex-roles and sexual identity in the Muslim world. *(See 62, 65, 494, 681).*

482.   Mernissi, Fatima. <u>The Veil and the Male Elite: A Feminist Interpretation of Women's Rights in Islam</u>. Reading: Addison Wesley Publishing Company, Inc. 1991.

An extraordinary book which travels back in time to trace the roots and significance of <u>Hadith</u> (tradition) in Islamic writings and culture. It talks about the subordination of women and also about women who stood up and were wonderful female role model. *(See 68).*

483.   Nazzal, Laila Ahed. <u>The Role of Shame in Societal Transformation among Palestinian Women on the West Bank</u>. Ph.D. Thesis. University of Pennsylvania, 1986.

Examines the moral order of Palestinian women of the West Bank and Jordan through the concept of "<u>aib</u>", shame, and its role in the social transformation of society. This concept is primarily concerned with the preservation of the ethical and proper conduct of societal members and is closely linked to the social institution of kinship. *(See 114, 126, 381).*

484.   Shaaban, Bouthaina.   Both Right and Left Hand: Arab
        Women Talk About Their Lives.   Bloomington: Indiana
        University Press, 1991.

This book encompasses a variety of Arab women's
experiences and questions the conception of the passive Arab
woman as portrayed in the media in the West.   The author
interviews a range of women: from poets to peasants, from
feminist activists to mothers of martyrs, from professors oppressed
at home to nomad matriarchs. *(See 74, 104, 691, 692).*

485.   Webster, Sheila K.   "Harim and Hijab: Seclusive and
        Exclusive Aspects of Traditional Muslim Dwelling and
        Dress."   Women's Studies International Forum 7, no. 4
        (1984): 251-57.

Architectural and clothing styles have been used to insulate
women from physical access to men outside their families.   This
article talks about some of the factors that contribute to this
segregation, and how women hold power in different ways. *(See
464, 467, 681).*

5.3 Women, State and Development Policies

486.   Afshar, Haleh.   "The Legal, Social and Political Position
        of Women in Iran."   International Journal of the Sociology
        of Law 13, no. 1 (February 1985): 47-60.

Discusses the political struggle of women for achieving
equality in 20th century Iran.   Iranian women have faced
overwhelming ideological obstacles. The emergence of the current
theocratic government has pushed women back to their position at
the beginning of the 20th century. *(See 114, 452, 472, 488).*

487.   Aghajanian, Akbar.   "The Impact of Development on the
        Status of Women: A District Level Analysis in Iran."

Journal of Developing Studies 7 (1991): 292-98.

Uses census data to measure the impact of development on women in Iran. Argues that gender stratification, together with class division, has an impact on women's lives. Examines women's access to education, health care, and paid employment and shows the existence of a strong inequality between women and men. *(See 501, 510).*

488. Bakhash, Haleh E. "Veil of Fears: Iran's Retreat from Women's Rights." New Republic 193, no. 18 (28 October 1985): 15-16.

Looks at the Islamic Republic of Iran's policy toward women and discusses briefly women's position under this theocratic regime. Of interest to researchers on women under Islam. *(See 474, 486).*

489. Bergmann, Barbara R., and Patricia J. Higgins. "Comment and Reply on Higgins's 'Women in the Islamic Republic of Iran: Legal, Social, and Ideological Changes." Signs 12, no. 3 (Spring 1987): 606-8.

An exchange of ideas on women's position in Iran between Barbara Bergmann and Patricia Higgins, two scholars of Iranian studies. *(See 493).*

490. Charrad, Mounira. "State and Gender in the Maghrib." Middle East Report 20, no. 2 (no. 163), (March-April 1990): 19-24.

Compares the position of women in three Maghrib countries and provides explanations for the difference in women's status. Shows the role of the State in bringing change. *(See 495).*

491. Fernea, Elizabeth. "Women and Family in Development Plans in the Arab East." Journal of Asian and African Studies 21, nos. 1-2 (Jan-April 1986): 81-88.

Development programs have ignored the diversity among
women as well as women's role in economic development in the
Middle East.   Therefore, women were not the beneficiaries of
development.   Development plans must be based on the actual
reality of developing countries and must address the central role of
women in the economy.

492.   Heggoy, Alf Andrew. "Cultural Disrespect: European and
        Algerian Views on Women in Colonial and Independent
        Algeria." The Muslim World LXII, no. 4 (October 1972):
        323-34.

Describes the attitudes of Algerians and Europeans towards
women within the context of antagonism between the colonizer and
the colonized. Looks at certain presuppositions held by each of the
societies which co-existed in colonial Algeria and which affected
the conception of women. *(See 72, 75, 99, 478, 687).*

493.   Higgins, Patricia J.   "Women in the Islamic Republic of
        Iran: Legal, Social, and Ideological Changes." Signs 10,
        no. 3 (Spring 1985): 477-94.

Compares the position of women in the Islamic Republic of
Iran with their position in the Pahlavi era, examining changes in
sex-role ideology, official rights and duties, and behavioural
patterns. Concludes that much of the reform during the Shah's
regime did not affect the majority of women. *(See 489).*

494.   Kandiyoti, Deniz A.   "Emancipated but Unliberated?
        Reflections on the Turkish Case." Feminist Studies 13, no.
        2 (Summer 1987): 317-38.

Identifies some of the factors accounting for similarities and
divergences in women's experiences in the Middle East.   It
demonstrates how the State can intervene to modify the place and
practice of Islam, and, consequently, the life options open to
women. *(See 62, 481, 537).*

495.   Kandiyoti, Deniz (ed.).   Women, Islam and the State.

London: Macmillan, 1991.

This book examines the relationship between Islam, the nature of state projects and the position of women in the modern nation states of the Middle East and South Asia. It argues that the political projects of these modern states, their specific national histories, and their interpretation of Islam are crucial for understanding the position of women in these states. *(See 451, 452, 490, 499, 688)*.

496.   Keddie, Nikki R.   "Iranian Revolutions in Comparative Perspective." The American Historical Review 88, no. 3 (June 1983): 579-98.

Discusses the historical roots of the Islamic Revolution in Iran and provides a comparative context for understanding this revolution. Shows the pros and cons of this revolution regarding its impact on the people who initially supported it. *(See 468)*.

497.   Marshall, Susan E., and Randall G. Stokes. "Tradition and the Veil: Female Status in Tunisia and Algeria." Journal of Modern African Studies 19, no. 4 (December 1981): 625-46.

Examines different government policies in two developing countries, Algeria and Tunisia, regarding women's status. Suggests that the degree of political instability, elite fragmentation, and ethnic revitalization largely account for the differences between government policies in these two countries. For these reasons, Algerian elites experienced a much stronger need for traditional legitimation than did the Tunisian elite. *(See 469, 482, 515, 687)*.

498.   Marshall, Susan E. "Paradoxes of Change: Culture Crisis, Islamic Revival, and the Reactivation of Patriarchy." Journal of Asian and African Studies 19, nos. 1-2 (January-April, 1984): 1-17.

Adopts a comparative perspective to explain the resurgence of Islamic patriarchy in Middle Eastern societies.   Certain conditions in these societies precipitate Islamic revival. Given the centrality of family in the Muslim world, increased constraint on women is the result of religious resurgence. *(See 321, 488, 496, 681)*.

499. Moghadam, Valentine M. Modernizing Women: Gender and Social Change in the Middle East. Boulder: Lynne Rienner Publishers, 1993.

The author focuses on the impact of change on the status of women in the Middle East and discusses women's role in the economy, family and social movements. She looks at the salient role of the state and demonstrates the centrality of the women's question in the process of change. *(See 451, 452, 495, 519, 681)*.

5.4 Work and Family

500. Afshar, Haleh. "Women in the Work and Poverty Trap in Iran." Capital and Class 37 (Spring 1981): 62-85.

Argues that the stated ideology of the present government in Iran stresses the domestic position of women. Women who are not "protected" by male heads of household and suffer from a poor economic position. This article analyzes the problem of poor women in Iran. *(See 240, 253, 508)*.

501. Aghajanian, Akbar. "Living Arrangements of Widows in Shiraz, Iran." Journal of Marriage and the Family 47, no. 3 (August 1985): 781-84.

Provides important information about widowhood as experienced by Iranian women. Shows that women with sons enjoy a far better standard of living than those who live on their own. *(See 487, 505)*.

502. Altorki, Soraya. Women in Saudi Arabia: Ideology and Behavior Among the Elite. New York: Columbia University Press, 1986.

This study focuses on elite domestic groups in Jiddah and attempts to discuss continuity and change among prominent Saudi Arabian families. It provides insights for understanding social change in domestic groups in the Middle Eastern Societies. *(See 450, 504, 524).*

503.   Brink, Judy H. "Changing Extended Family Relationships in an Egyptian Village." Urban Anthropology 16, no. 2 (Summer 1987): 133-49.

It is recognized that development reduces the power of old people in the extended family. However, this paper argues that in this Egyptian village development has affected men and women differently. This paper discusses the dynamics of power relations within the family in rural areas. *(See 458, 501, 686).*

504.   Butler, Alan. "Sexual Apartheid in Saudi Arabia." New Society 45 (July 6, 1978): 13-15.

A British teacher of English as a second language in Anaizah, in 1970, gives his account of women in Saudi Arabia. He sheds light on the Saudi enclosed society, and on the patriarchal structure of family, religion, and state. *(See 450, 502, 524).*

505.   Hablemitoglu, Sengul, and Emine Gonen. "Elderly Women in Turkey: An Economic Viewpoint." International Journal of Sociology of the Family 21, no. 1 (Spring 1991): 85-96.

Looks at the problems that elderly women from different groups face. Concludes that women from the lower income groups confront more difficulties. *(See 480, 501).*

506.   Haeri, Shahla. The Law of Desire: Temporary Marriage in Iran. London: I.B. Tauris, 1990.

A scholarly analysis of temporary marriage, one of the most important practices affecting the lives of women in many Muslim countries. The author focuses on Iran and provides a thorough discussion of the controversial issue of temporary marriage. *(See 468, 471, 688)*.

507.   Kagitcibasi, Cigdem. "Status of Women in Turkey: Cross-Cultural Perspectives." International Journal of Middle East Studies 18 (1986): 485-99.

Deals with the private sphere of women's lives, mainly in the family. Compares Turkish women's status in the family with the baseline of Middle Eastern-Eastern Mediterranean family culture. Points to the complexity as well as differences and similarities among various male dominated cultures. *(See 457, 505)*.

508.   Kordi, Gohar. An Iranian Odyssey. London: Serpant's Tail, 1991.

A Kurdish woman's autobiography and her personal struggle in various stages of life. An outstanding story of growing up as a Kurdish woman. *(See 474, 500)*.

509.   Mir-Hosseini, Ziba. "Impact of Wage Labour on Household Fission in Rural Iran." Journal of Comparative Family Studies 18, no. 3 (Autumn 1987): 445-61.

Discusses the diversity in the household structure regarding the ownership of resources and the work relations involved in using these resources. Various groups in the village have 'ideals' of family relations, but they differ significantly in their realization of these ideals. *(See 452, 458, 513)*.

510.   Molyneux, Maxine. "Legal Reform and Socialist Revolution in Democratic Yemen: Women and the Family." International Journal of the Sociology of Law 13, no. 2 (May 1985): 147-72.

Describes the transformation in the juridical system after independence in Yemen. It demonstrates how legal reform constituted an integral part of transforming the economy and regulating social relations within the family. These changes are seen as necessary by the government for realizing its development goals. *(See 452, 487, 495).*

511.   Nassehi-Behnam, Vida. "Change and the Iranian Family." Current Anthropology 26, no. 5 (December 1985): 557-62.

Discusses the impact of socio-economic changes on the Iranian family. Despite changes, the Iranian family has kept several aspects of its traditional functions. Provides a typology of family in Iran. *(See 503, 508).*

512.   Papanek,   Hanna.   "Class   and   Gender   in Education-Employment Linkages." Comparative Education Review 29, no. 3 (August 1985): 317-46.

Proposes that the interplay between the household and the labour market determines female educational and labour force participation.   Family strategies of educational investment, response to changes in labour demand, and the female labour requirement within and outside households can be understood in terms of the relationship between the family and the larger economy. Illustrates particular aspects of educational-employment linkages by examining specific data on Egypt and Bangladesh. *(See 264, 473).*

513.   Tucker, Judith, Mona Hammam, et al. Special issue of Merip Reports on "Women and Work in the Middle East." Merip Reports no.95 (March-April 1981).

This issue of **MERIP** contains a number of important articles which address various aspects of women's life in the Middle East, including women's position in the household and labour market. It questions the stereotypical views of women in Middle Eastern societies. *(See 458, 500, 509, 517, 681, 686).*

5.5 Women's Experience of Wage-Work

514.   Bernstein, Deborah.   "Economic Growth and Female
        Labour: The Case of Israel." Sociological Review 31, no.
        2 (May 1983): 263-292.

    The growth of the economy and the demand for two
incomes have brought an increasing number of women into the
labour market in Israel. This paper examines the main features of
the economic growth and the position of women in various
branches of the economy.   The sexual division of labour is
analyzed according to the differences between Ashkenazi and
Oriental women. As well, the author assesses their contribution and
future position in the labour force. *(See 513, 520, 550).*

515.   Gallissot, Rene.   "L'Etat-relais a partir de l'exemple
        algerien. La transnationalisation a l'oeuvre sous le modele
        de l'Etat national." Peuples Mediterraneans nos. 35-36
        (avril-septembre 1986): 247-56.

    Focuses on Algeria to argue that the newly nationalist and
independent Third World countries promote transnationalization
through State apparatus. This process swells works in the tertiary
sector which enhances the polarization between male and female in
the labour force. *(See 497, 499, 538, 682).*

516.   Hatem, Mervat.   "Egypt's Middle Class in Crisis: The
        Sexual Division of Labor." Middle East Journal 42, no. 3
        (Summer 1988): 407-22.

    Discusses the rise of a new conservative middle class in
Egypt. The nationalist patriarchal system has accommodated this
newly emerging conservative wing. The commitment of this
alliance to gender equality is questionable. It is argued that these
patriarchal alliances have prevented women from organizing an
effective women's movement. *(See 458, 503, 513, 529, 686).*

517.   Meleis, Afaf Ibrahim.   "Effect of Modernization on
        Kuwaiti Women." Social Science and Medicine 16, no. 9
        (1982): 965-970.

Explores the impact of modernization on women in Kuwaiti and shows that women confront conflictory values. On the one hand, modernization improved education and occupational opportunities for women; on the other hand, women face conservative traditional restrictions. *(See 452, 455, 526)*.

518. Mernissi, Fatima. Beyond the Veil: Male-Female Dynamics in Modern Muslim Society (Revised Edition). Bloomington: Indiana University Press, 1987.

The author argues that the present conservative wave against women in the Muslim countries is a defense against recent changes in sex-roles. It shows that modernity is incompatible with traditional Muslim structures and discusses the ensuing contradictions pervading nearly all Muslim societies. *(See 451, 499, 514)*.

519. Moghadam, Val. "Women, work and Ideology in the Islamic Republic." International Journal of Middle East Studies 20 (1988): 221-43.

The author examines the impact of patriarchal Islamic ideology on women's economic role in Iran and shows that the Islamic ideology of domesticity has not been successful and that women play an important role in the capitalist economy. The regime's discriminatory policies toward women could have a unifying effect on urban women. *(See 114, 488, 495, 499)*.

520. Moskoff, William. "Women and Work in Israel and the Islamic Middle East." Quarterly Review of Economics and Business 22, no. 4 (Winter 1982): 89-104.

Examines the labour force status of women in Israel and Islamic countries of the Middle East. The focus is on the determinants of labour force participation. There are significant differences between Israel and Middle Eastern countries in this regard. *(See 498, 514, 526)*.

521.   Pedersen, Birgitte Rahbek. "Arab Women." Folk 21-22
        (1979-1980): 63-71

Criticizes the stereotypical presentation of Arab women as
being passive and in veil. Presents a short discussion of Arab
women's role in production. *(See 455, 462, 523).*

522.   Peterson, J. E. "The Political Status of Women in Arab
        Gulf States." Middle East Journal 43, no. 1 (Winter 1989):
        34-50.

Argues that despite appearances, women play an essential
political role in the Gulf States. Education has been a major
source of change and recent trends have brought more women to
paid employment. Social change is contributing to the growth of
women's opportunities. At the same time, neoconservatism and
the return to veil is gaining importance among women. *(See 455,
460, 523).*

523.   Ramazani, Nesta. "Arab Women in the Gulf." The
        Middle East Journal 39, no. 2 (Spring 1985): 258-276.

The Iranian Revolution had an impact on the lives of
women in the Gulf States and there has been a return to strict
Islamic values. This paper argues that a close examination shows
that significant changes took place in women's status and their
position. *(See 455, 462, 521).*

524.   Rawaf, Monirah. "The Changing Status of Women in
        Management in the Public Administration of Saudi Arabia."
        Public Administration and Development 10, no. 2 (April-
        June 1990): 209-219.

Provides a brief account of women's participation in the
public administration in Saudi Arabia. Uses interviews to cite
obstacles that women most commonly face in working outside the
home. Provides suggestions for reform. *(See 450, 502, 504).*

525.   Rockwell, Susan. "Palestinian Women Workers in the

Israeli-Occupied Gaza Strip." Journal of Palestine Studies
14, no. 2(54) (Winter 1985): 114-36.

Uses the notions of gender and social class to discuss
women workers' discrimination in the Gaza Strip. Discusses the
cultural factors which discourage Arab women from entering the
labour market. Women wage-workers are poor, have subordinate
position, and are discriminated against both politically and
economically. *(See 463, 513, 514, 520, 692).*

526.   Sanad, Jamal A., and Mark A. Tessler. "The Economic
        Orientations of Kuwaiti Women: Their Nature,
        Determinants, and Consequences." International Journal of
        Middle East Studies 20 (1988): 443-68.

Uses a sample of over five hundred to discuss issues which
face women in Kuwait. Provides revealing statistics on women's
participation in the labour force and women's own thoughts about
various aspects of their lives. *(See 517).*

527.   Shaw, R. Paul.   "Women's Employment in the Arab
        World: A Strategy of Selective Intervention." Development
        and Change 12 (1981): 237-71.

Criticizes the commonly held notion about Arab women
being "culturally enslaved" or "economically exploited." Looks at
the liberating effects of economic development, progressive legal
reforms, and feminist movements on Arab women's position in
society. Calls for policies which put women's emancipation on the
top of the agenda. *(See 460, 513, 536, 540).*

528.   Soffan, Linda U. "The Role of Women in the Economy of
        the United Arab Emirates." Labour and Society 5, no. 1
        (January 1980): 3-17.

Discusses women's position in the labour market in the
United Arab Emirates. Shows very clearly the impact of tradition
and Islamic ideology on the lives of women. Despite changes in the
twentieth century, there is continuity in women's status and roles.

(See 455, 465).

529.   Taplin, Ruth.   "Women and Work in Egypt: A Social
        Historical Perspective." International Sociology 2, no. 1
        (March 1987): 61-76.

        Questions theories of women's work in the Muslim Arab
world.   Provides historical evidence from Egypt to show that
Muslim women have always participated in the labour force, both
on an informal and formal basis.   This paper discusses various
types of work done by different classes of women in the five stages
of Egypt's economic development. *(See 460, 516, 527, 540, 636).*

530.   Weiss, Anita M.   "Tradition and Modernity at the
        Workplace: A Field Study of Women in the Pharmaceutical
        Industry of Lahore." Women's Studies International Forum
        7, no. 4 (1984): 259-64.

        This paper investigates how modernity and tradition are
reconciled in women's work in the factory and how "purdah"
ideology is adjusted to the needs of production. *(See 451, 499).*

5.6 Working in the Rural Areas

531.   Abu-Lughod, Lila.   "A Community of Secrets: The
        Separate World of Bedouin Women." Signs 10, no. 4
        (Summer 1985): 637-57.

        This paper discusses the life of Bedouin women. It argues
that women spend much of their time apart from men living in a
separate world and form some sort of community within the larger
society. This community is a rich world of close ties. *(See 57,
468, 533, 693).*

532.   Afshar, Haleh.   "The Position of Women in an Iranian
        Village." Feminist Review no. 9 (Autumn 1981): 78-86.

        Discusses women's role in production in one Iranian village

and case study and shows that the participation of women in socially productive work may result in their further subordination rather than their liberation. *(See 472, 493).*

533.   Beck, Lois.   Nomad: A Year in the Life of a Qashqa'i Tribesman of Iran. London: I.B. Touris, 1991.

This book provides an account of a well-known Persian tribe and their day-to-day activities- from private to public, and from sacred to mundane events.   An essential reading for understanding tribal life. *(See 531, 541, 693).*

534.   Dickerscheid, Jean D.   "Profiles of Rural Egyptian Women: Rules, Status and Needs," International Journal of Sociology of the Family 20, 1 (Spring 1990): 1-20.

Provides a general description of rural women's lives in Egypt.   Addresses rural women's role in the family, their education, employment and health problems.   The author provides recommendations to improve women's status. *(See 535).*

535.   El Saadawi, Nawal. God Dies By the Nile. London: Zed Books, 1985.

This novel illustrates the class dimension of the oppression of women in a village on the banks of the Nile.   The story is a simple and tragic one.   It can be seen as a metaphor for the Sadat regime and landlords' oppression in general. *(See 73, 534).*

536.   Hopkins, Nicholas S.   "Women, Work and Wages in Two Arab Villages." Eastern Anthropologist 44, no. 2 (1992): 103-23.

Focuses on the symbolism of female specificity and attempts to see how it is portrayed in two villages in Tunisia and Egypt. Relates the symbolism of gender differences to distinctions in status and class, and shows how symbolism plays a role in maintaining the socio-economic structures of these two communities. *(See 460, 521, 527).*

537.   Kandiyoti, Deniz. "Economie monetaire et roles des sexes:
        le cas de la Turquie." Current Sociology 31, no. 1 (Spring
        1983): 213-29.

Discusses the impact of rural transformation on women in
Turkey. The incorporation into the market economy had deep
impacts on households. While the wives of capitalist farmers
retreated from production, women in small-holding households
intensified their work. In areas of heavy male migration, we see
the feminization of agriculture. *(See 457, 494, 539)*.

538.   Schnetzler, Jacques. "Les effets pervers du sous-emploi à
        travers l'exemple algérien." Revue canadienne des études
        africaines/Canadian Journal of African Studies 14, no. 3
        (1980): 451-71.

Algeria's development plans involved a huge investment in
building factories and industrial complexes. These programs
neglected the rural population and proved to be unprofitable. They
resulted in high unemployment and a rural exodus of the
population. Development programs benefited a small fraction of
men employed in the industrial and service sectors and
marginalized women and the rural labour force. *(See 497, 499,
515)*.

539.   Starr, June. "The Role of Turkish Secular Law in
        Changing the Lives of Rural Muslim Women, 1950-1970."
        Law and Society Review 23, no. 3 (August 1989): 497-
        523.

This article argues that political reforms and legal
intervention have improved women's situation and guaranteed them
of certain rights. It questions the image of passive Muslim women
and shows rural women were active in changing their lives. *(See
457, 494, 537)*.

540.   Sukkary-Stolba, Soheir. "Changing Roles of Women in
        Egypt's Newly Reclaimed Lands." Anthropological
        Quarterly 58, no. 4 (October 1985): 182-189.

Focuses on the impact on women of migration to the newly reclaimed lands in Egypt. Shows that migration affected various groups of women differently and discusses their workloads, social mobility, and public participation. Shows the active participation of Moslem women in building communities. *(See 527, 529).*

541. Tapper, Nancy. "Matrons and Mistresses: Women and Boundaries in Two Middle Eastern Tribal Societies." Archives Europeenes de Sociologie 21, no. 1 (1980): 59-79.

The author attempts to explain women's position in two different tribal societies. She suggests that in light of the considerable economic and cultural similarities between these two societies, economic factors alone are not able to explain differences in the position of women. There is a need to examine features of the social structure and wider social environment. *(See 472, 531, 533).*

5.7 Working for Change

542. Ahmed, Leila. "Feminism and Feminist Movements in the Middle East, A Preliminary Exploration: Turkey, Egypt, Algeria, People's Democratic Republic of Yemen." Women's Studies International Forum 5, no. 2 (1982): 153-68.

Attempts to analyze women's status in a number of Islamic Middle Eastern societies with different cultures and histories: women's position differs and feminism is received differently in these countries. *(See 61, 65, 496, 681).*

543. Azad, Shahrzad. "Workers' and Peasants' Councils in Iran." Monthly Review 32, no. 5 (October 1980): 14-29.

Discusses the formation and activities of the peasants' and workers' councils in Iran after the Revolution as an example of spontaneous grassroots movement and people's rule. Discusses the reasons for the movement's set back. *(See 496, 519).*

544.   El Guindi, Fadwa.   "Veiling Infitah with Muslim Ethic:
        Egypt's   Contemporary   Islamic   Movement."   Social
        Problems 28, no. 4 (April 1981): 465-85.

This paper argues that a community of new Egyptian
women is emerging and has the apparent contradictions of being
modern, college-educated, and career-oriented, yet is apparently
fundamentalist and veiled. This new type of woman represents a
larger movement and the veil is a symbol which has complex
interactions with infrastructural changes. *(See 477, 498, 681).*

545.   Ertürk, Yakin.   "Convergence and Divergence in the Status
        of Moslem Women: The Cases of Turkey and Saudi
        Arabia."   International Sociology 6, no. 3 (September
        1991): 307-320.

The problem of women in Muslim countries is not gaining
the right to enter the public domain, but requires conscious changes
at all levels of society.   Women's liberation is not a religious
problem but a political one. *(See 450, 494).*

546.   Fahmy, Hoda Youssef.   "Building Upon Tradition: A
        Women's Handicraft Project in Upper Egypt." Assignment
        Children 49-50 (Spring 1980): 197-206.

Describes an income-generating handicraft project for
women in Egypt. Not only did this project give women a chance
to have a source of income for themselves, it also allowed them to
acquire management and other types of skills. The success of a
project is due to its compatability with traditional cultural patterns.
(See 354, 363).

547.   Ferchiou, Sophie.   "Pouvoir, contre-pouvoir et société en
        mutation: L'exemple tunisien." Peuples méditerraneéns/
        Mediterranean Peoples nos. 48-49 (juillet-decembre. 1989):
        81-92.

Points to the fact that Tunisia is among the countries in which the State introduced measures to reduce inequalities between women and men. Distinguishes between the power basis of women in rural and urban areas. Concludes that each form of masculine domination has a corresponding counter feminine power and resistance. *(See 490, 495, 687)*.

548. Milani, Farzaneh. Veils and Words: The Emerging Voices of Iranian Women Writers. London: I.B. Tauris, 1992.

The author provides a rich historical account of Iranian women who broke the silence and contributed to a great literary tradition. She presents a fascinating discussion of the problems that these women faced and the social costs associated with their action. *(See 464, 478, 552)*.

549. Peteet, Julie M. Gender in Crisis: Women and the Palestinian Resistance Movement. New York: Columbia University Press, 1991.

This study sketches a portrait of "ordinary" camp women and politically active Palestinian women in Lebanon: the emergence of their political consciousness and its relation to feminist consciousness, how they are mobilized into political organizations and the tasks they perform, and what political activism implies for the concept of gender. *(See 459, 463, 525, 692)*.

550. Shaarawi, Huda. Harem Years: The Memoirs of an Egyptian Feminist (1879-1924). Translated by Margot Badran. New York: Feminist Press at the City University of New York, 1986.

Harem Years is the memoirs of an early Egyptian feminist and nationalist. A moving description of Huda Shaarawi's personal life and the problems and limitations which faced her as a woman. Despite impediments, Shaarawi eventually succeeded to gain women's leadership. *(See 61)*.

551.   Shamgar-Handelman, Lea. <u>Israeli War Widows: Beyond the Glory of Heroism</u>.   Mass.: Bergin and Garvey Publishers, Inc., 1986.

This book is about one of the lesser known casualties of war, war widows. It discusses the problems of adjustment to war-widowhood. *(See 514, 682)*.

552.   Tabari, Azar.   "The Women's Movement in Iran: A Hopeful Prognosis." <u>Feminist Studies</u> 12, no. 2 (Summer 1986): 343-60.

Focuses on the emergence of the women's movement in Iran immediately after the overthrow of the Shah's regime.   At present, the women's movement carries a tremendous weight in challenging Islam as a governmental system. *(See 548)*.

Chapter Six

Audiovisual Resources

6.1 General

553. <u>A Woman's Place</u>. 25 minutes, video. Vancouver: T.H.A Media, 1988.

This documentary presents an impressive pastiche of women who have influenced the course of current events in the world.

554. <u>Abortion: Stories From North and South</u>. 54 minutes, 16mm/video. Montreal: National Film Board of Canada, 1984

This film provides an historical overview of how the church, state and the medical establishment have influenced policies concerning abortion. It refers to Ireland, Japan, Colombia, Peru and Canada. *(See 239)*.

555. <u>Bitter Cane</u>. 75 minutes, 16mm, video. Toronto: Full Frame Film and Video Distribution, 1983.

This film shows the transformation of traditional agriculture and the growth of foreign-owned plantations. The focus in on Haiti, but the subject matter is applicable to many Third World countries. *(See 16, 24, 159)*.

556. <u>Catalyst Media Review: An Annotated Bibliography of</u>

Audiovisuals on Women and Work. (Quarterly magazine with annual index). New York: Catalyst Media.

This review provides descriptive information and comments on audiovisuals on women in a wide-range of work-related issues. *(See 579)*.

557.   Children in Debt (Ninos Deudores). 30 minutes, 16mm. Vancouver: International Development Education Resource Association, 1987.

This film examines the impact of austerity measures that have been imposed by the IMF on social services and the living conditions of people, especially children.   The focus is on Argentina, Bolivia, Colombia and Peru, but it is applicable to many Third World counties. *(See 25, 26, 377, 402)*.

558.   Cost of Cotton. 30 minutes, 16mm.   Vancouver: International Development Education Resource Association, 1979.

This documentary is about the impact of the international demand for cotton on developing nations, in general and on Guatemala, in particular. *(See 6)*.

559.   Cultivating Famine: The World Food Crisis. 30 minutes, slide tape.   Vancouver: International Development Education Resource Association, 1975.

This slide tape looks at the historical and structural causes of the world food crisis and their commonly advocated solutions. *(See 15, 23, 26)*.

560.   The Debt Crisis-New Perspectives. 55 minutes, video. New York: Filmaker Library, 1989.

This video brings out the complexities of the debt crisis and its impact on both developed and developing countries. *(See 25, 557)*.

561. The Economics Game. 12 minutes, video. Ottawa: Canadian International Development Agency, 1977.

This video shows the current economic system works to the detriment of the Third World. *(See 23).*

562.   Focus on women. 28 minutes, video. Ottawa: Canadian International Development Agency, 1980.

This video uses examples from India, Egypt, and the Dominican Republic to explore the visual media's stereotyping of women and their role in society. *(See 58).*

563.   Global Assembly Line.   58 minutes, 16mm/video. Toronto: Full Frame Film and Video Distribution, 1986.

This documentary takes the viewer inside the global economy and shows the lives of women who work in the 'free trade zones' in the Third World. *(See 2, 403,415, 495).*

564.   Hungry For Profit.   85 minutes, video.   Vancouver: International Development Education Resource Association, 1985.

This video focuses on agribusiness, investigating the roots of hunger and the difficulties that face the direct agricultural producers. *(See 24, 159, 555).*

565.   Increase and Multiply? 55 minutes, video. New York: Filmakers Library, 1989.

This documentary examines the devastating impacts of population growth on the Third World countries. *(See 13, 186, 396, 624).*

566.   Journey For Survival. 15 minutes, video. Ottawa: Canadian International Development Agency, 1981.

This video documents the journey of women in the Third

World in their search for clean water. *(See 2, 12, 28).*

567.   Key Women At International Women's Year. 29 minutes,
       video. N.Y.: Stuart (Martha) Communications, Inc. 1975.

       This video presents the discussion that was held among
women leaders who attended the 1975 Mexico City women's
conference. *(See 74, 144, 149).*

568.   Making Do. 50 minutes, 16mm/video. Toronto: Full
       Frame Film and Video Distribution, 1990.

       This documentary was filmed in Nepal, Peru and Senegal
and shows the resourcefulness of Third World people in developing
an informal economy. *(See 178, 296, 391, 419).*

569.   The   Money   Lenders: The   World   Bank   and   The
       International   Monetary   Fund.   85   minutes,   video.
       Vancouver: International Development Education Resource
       Association, 1992.

       The focus of this documentary is on Bolivia, Ghana, Brazil,
Thailand and the Philippines, and it shows the role of the IMF and
the World Bank in the Third World Countries. *(See 25, 26, 280,
649).*

570.   Mothers in Conflict--Children in Need.   25 minutes,
       16mm. Chicago: Scientificom Audiovisual, 1979.

       This audio-visual Examines the plight of mothers and
infants in the Third World. *(See 2, 19, 72, 114, 453).*

571.   The Operation. 32 minutes, video. Winnipeg: IDEA
       Centre. 1983

       A discussion of how methods of reproductive control have
been forced on women is the focus of this video. *(See 239, 554).*

572.   Paths of Development: Behind the Image.   30 minutes,

video. Hull: Canadian International Development Agency, 1985.

This video shows how the Third World's development goals relate to those of the industrialized countries. The focus is on Malaysia, Peru and Niger. *(See 1, 18, 23).*

573. Paths of Development: Days of Future Past. 30 minutes, video. Hull: Canadian International Development Agency, 1985.

Focusing on Malaysia, Peru and Niger, this video examines the origin of conflict between the industrialized and the Third World countries. *(See 25, 29, 30, 265, 385).*

574. Paths of Development: Justice for All. 30 minutes, video. Hull: Canadian International Development Agency, 1985.

This video focuses on Peru, Malaysia and Niger, and addresses fundamental issues faced by developing countries in implementing their development strategies. *(See 2, 114, 453).*

575. Paths of Development: The Monster Machine. 30 minutes, video. Hull: Canadian International Development Agency, 1985.

This video looks at the interdependence of the global economy, and explores several factors which are beyond the control of the poor nations and which work against their interests. *(See 14, 15, 18, 23, 25, 26).*

576. Paths of Development: Striking a Balance. 30 minutes, video. Hull: Canadian International Development Agency, 1985.

This video examines the tough questions that the Third World countries must address in order to achieve development. *(See 6, 15, 17, 22).*

577.   Speaking of Nairobi. 56 minutes, 16mm/video. Montreal:
        National Film Board, 1986.

        This film is devoted to the international women's
movement. This four part package draws attention to the
differences between the developed and underdeveloped nations.
(See 567).

578.   Starving for Sugar: The Human Story Behind Sugar and the
        Bio-technology Revolution. 57 minutes, video.
        Vancouver: International Development Education Resource
        Association, 1988.

        This documentary tells the story of the collapse of the sugar
cane industry and recounts the human tragedy that has resulted
from the bio-technological revolution. *(See 3, 176, 306, 340)*.

579.   Sullivan, Kay. Films, For, By and About Women. New
        Jersey: The Scarecrow Press, Inc. 1985.

        This book provides about 3200 titles and is meant to
complement the previous volume published in 1980. *(See 556)*.

580.   Women: All One Nation. 28 minutes, video. Winnipeg:
        IDEA Centre (no date).

        This film looks at women's global inequality, and makes
connections between women living in industrialized nations and
those of the Third World. *(See 2, 154, 239, 368, 451)*.

581.   The World Challenge: Inter-Connected Worlds. 50
        minutes, video. Hull: Canadian International Development
        Agency, 1986.

        This video investigates the positive and negative facets of
the interdependence between developed and developing nations.
(See 1, 6, 12, 19, 23, 239).

582.   The World Challenge: The World Challenge. 50 minutes,

video. Hull: Canadian International Development Agency, 1986.

This video provides a factual look at the computer era and relates computers to the issue of Third World poverty. *(See 6, 23, 204)*.

6.2 Africa

583. Africa: Volume IV. 106 minutes, video. Toronto: T.H.A. Media Distributors, 1990.

This video charts Africa's nationalism and the rise of the independence movement. *(See 154, 172, 235)*.

584. Angola is our Country. 45 minutes, video. Vancouver: International Development Education Resource Association, 1988.

Women speak at length about the legal status of women in Angola. *(See 74, 144, 189, 598, 623)*.

585. Asante Market Women. 52 minutes, video. New York: Filmakers Library, 1983.

Focusing on Ghana, this video demonstrates the power of women in the market-place. *(See 199, 204, 205, 590)*.

586. Awake from Mourning . 50 minutes, video. Seattle: Villion Films, 1982.

Three women struggle against the indignities of South Africa's racial policies in this video. *(See 154, 158, 198, 204)*.

587. Becoming a Woman in Okrika. 27 minutes, video. New York: Filmakers Library, 1991.

This documentary reveals the conflict that women in Okrika

face between their traditional customs and the values of the modern 'outside' world. *(See 3, 17, 78, 176)*.

588.   Crossroads/ South Africa.   50 minutes, 16mm.   San Francisco: California Newsreel, 1981.

This film looks at the illegal squatters' settlement which was built by the wives of Capetown's black workers. *(See 154, 589, 591, 602)*.

589.   The Cry of Reason--Beyers Naude: An Afrikaner Speaks Out.   56 minutes, 16mm.   Vancouver: International Development Education Resource Association, 1989.

This documentary shows the power of hope and commitment, and people's capacity to change. *(See 154, 588, 591)*.

590.   Fair Trade.   27 minutes, video.   Montreal: National Film Board of Canada, 1990.

This film focuses on Tanzania and is about women's venture into the market-place. *(See 199, 204, 205, 585)*.

591.   Forget Not Our Sisters.   39 minutes, slide tape. Cambridge: American Friends Service Committee, 1982.

This slide show offers a powerful tribute to the courage of South African women. *(See 154, 235, 588, 589, 602)*.

592.   From The Shore.   16 minutes, video.   Montreal: National Film Board of Canada, 1990.

A group of women engaged in a thriving fish business in a Muslim village in Kenya are documented in this video. *(See 227, 230)*.

593.   Journey to Understanding.   90 minutes, video.   Hull: Canadian International Development Agency, 1990.

This series of six 15 minute educational programs explores the key development issues facing Africa today. *(See 154, 159, 162, 168, 176)*.

594.   The Liberation of Women in Guinea-Bissau. 16 minutes, slide tape. Toronto: Development Education Centre, 1979.

This program explains the changes that have taken place in the position of women since independence in Guinea-Bissau. *(See 154, 179, 591)*.

595.   Maids and Madams. 52 minutes, video. Toronto: Full Frame Film and Video Distribution, 1985.

The painful relations between black maids and white madams in today's South Africa are examined in this film. *(See 198)*.

596.   Man-Made Famine. 52 minutes, video. Vancouver: International Development Education Resource Association, 1986.

This video presents the stories of three women from three African countries- Kenya, Zimbabwe and Burkina Faso- who tell of their struggle to feed their families. *(See 13, 16, 159, 183, 648)*.

597.   Mozambique: The Struggle for Survival. 57 minutes, video. Vancouver: International Development Education Resource Association, 1987.

This video provides the reviewer with the vital information which is needed to understand the key issues in Southern Africa. *(See 172, 179)*.

598.   Msai Women. 51 minutes, 16mm. Philadelphia: Ishi Films, 1979.

This film is about women of the Msai tribe from childhood,

through marriage, to old age. *(See 74, 144, 584, 623).*

599.   Naked Spaces: Living is Round.   136 minutes, 16mm.
       Vancouver: International Development Education Resource
       Association, 1985.

       A feature-length documentary on various aspects of
women's lives in Western Africa. *(See 154, 584, 598).*

600.   Nyamakuta- the One Who Receives: An African Midwife.
       32 minutes, video. New York: Filmakers Library, 1989.

       May Mafuta is a nyamakuta- a traditional midwife- in
Zimbabwe. Women like her attend half of the births in developing
countries.

601.   Reassemblage.   40   minutes,   16mm.   Vancouver:
       International Development Education Resource Association,
       1983.

       A documentary on women in Senegal which challenges the
ethnocentrism underlying Western anthropological studies of 'other'
cultures. *(See 43, 71).*

602.   South Africa Belongs to Us: The Struggle of Black Women
       of South Africa.   57 minutes, 16mm.   New York: Icarus
       Films, 1980.

       A film on the lives of black women in South Africa. *(See
154, 235, 588, 589).*

603.   Water for Tonoumasse.   28 minutes, video.   New York:
       Filmakers Library, 1988.

       This video tells us about women's daily lives in
Tonoumasse and their efforts to get clean water. *(See 74, 144,
154, 584).*

604.   Weaving our Lives: Tapestries Reflect Life in Botswana.

25 minutes, slide tape. Toronto: Participatory Research Group, 1979.

This slide tape comes with a 50 page booklet and explores such themes as rural development, everyday life and the position of men and women in African society. *(See 2, 113, 160).*

605.   When the Mountains Tremble. 83 minutes, video. New York: New Yorker Films, 1983.

A vigorous documentary that describes the peasants struggle against oppression. *(See 182, 235).*

606.   Where Credit is Due. 27 minutes, video. Montreal: National Film Board, 1990.

This film looks at the issue of women's access to credit. *(See 227).*

607.   With These Hands. 33 minutes, video. New York: Filmakers Library, 1987.

Three women from Kenya, Zimbabwe and Burkino Faso tell of their struggle to feed their families. *(See 218, 219, 230).*

608.   Women At Work. 50 minutes, video. Vancouver: International Development Education Resource Association, 1989.

This documentary looks at the devastating impact of land erosion on the largely agrarian population of Kenya and discusses women's mobilization, in this process. *(See 182, 235, 605).*

609.   You Have Struck A Rock. 30 minutes, video. Toronto: Full Frame Film and Video Distribution, 1981.

This film documents women's resistance to the 'pass' laws in South Africa. *(See 235, 608).*

6.3 Asia

610. A Handle on Health. 27 minutes, video. Montreal:
      National Film Board of Canada, 1986 .

      This video looks at the development projects in Ethiopia,
Malaysia, the Philippines, Sri Lanka and Thailand that help ensure
a reliable water supply for women.

611. After the Difficulties: Working Women in Southeast Asia.
      18 minutes, Slide show. Toronto: Development Education
      Centre, 1982.

      This slide show looks at Asian women who leave their rural
homes in search of work in the cities, many of whom find work in
micro-tech plants run by international corporations. *(See 10, 611).*

612. All Under Heaven. 60 minutes, 16mm/video. New Jersey:
      Full Frame Video and Film Distribution, 1986.

      This film provides an intimate look at daily life in Long
Bow, a village 400 miles South West of Beijing. *(See 355, 357,
630).*

613. China's Only Child. 60 minutes, video. London: British
      Broadcasting Company, 1984.

      This video looks at the program that was used to control
population growth in China and how it was administered. *(See
243, 263, 334).*

614. Dadi's Family. 58 minutes, video. Alexandria: PBS
      Video 1981.

      This video offers an intimate portrait of rural women who
live in a family facing crisis. *(See 330, 331, 337).*

615. The Great Wall of Tradition. 27 minutes, video.
      Montreal: National Film Board of Canada, 1988.

Insight into a societal contradiction in modern China is provided by this video. *(See 243, 263, 355, 636).*

616.   Holding Our Ground.   50   minutes,   16mm/video. Montreal: National Film Board of Canada, 1988.

This film looks at a group of women who have organized and put pressure on their government to implement land reform. *(See 24, 363).*

617.   India Cabaret. 60 minutes, 16mm. New York: Filmakers Library, 1988.

This film focuses on female strippers who work in a night club in the suburb of Bombay. *(See 246, 253, 257).*

618.   Islam and Feminism.   25 minutes, video.   New York: Icarus Films, 1991.

This report examines the position of women in Pakistan. *(See 260, 276, 634).*

619.   Kababaihan: Filipina Portraits.   40   minutes,   video. Vancouver International Development Education Resource Association, 1989.

This video presents a portrait of some of the women's involvement in grassroots organization in the Philippines. *(See 237, 250, 280).*

620.   Kheturni Bayo: North Indian Farm Women.   19 minutes, 16mm.   San Francisco: San Francisco Matching Service, 1980.

This audiovisual offers an introduction to the daily life of peasant women in Western India. *(See 332, 337, 348).*

621.   Lifting the Blackout: Images of North Korea. 54 minutes, video. Toronto: International Tele-film, 1989.

This documentary examines the history, politics and culture of North Korea, including the status of the women living in that country. *(See 628)*.

622.   Marginal People.   28 minutes, 16mm.   Pullman: Washington State University, 1978.

This film provides a picture of the dire living conditions of the people of Bangladesh. *(See 240, 248, 276, 279, 291)*.

623.   Masteri- A Balinese Woman.   78 minutes, 16mm. Burbank: Avis Films, 1975.

An exploration into the day-to-day activities of a Balinese couple is provided in this audio-visual. *(See 74, 144, 584, 598)*.

624.   3900 Million and One.   50 minutes, video.   London: British Broadcasting Company, 1974.

This film examines a number of problems facing development in rural India. *(See 13, 186, 332, 337, 396, 565)*.

625.   Modernization...But for Whom?.   15 minutes, video. Vancouver: International Development Education Resource Association, 1988.

This video provides a critical look at the Malaysian government's modernization policy. *(See 239, 273, 301)*.

626.   No Longer Silent.   56 minutes, 16mm/video.   Montreal: National Film Board of Canada, 1986.

This film examines the plight of women in India struggling against injustices. *(See 240, 244, 288, 532, 637, 640)*.

627.   Old World, New Women.   28 minutes, 16mm.   Los Angeles: Chinese Information Service, 1975.

This film offers its viewers a picture of women's role in

modern China. *(See 243, 315, 335, 615).*

628. The Pacific Era. 25 minutes, Slide tape. Vancouver: International Development Education Resource Association, 1981.

This slide tape show provides a picture of the economic and political development of the Pacific Basin. *(See 14, 302, 621).*

629. Perhaps Women Are More Economical. 27 minutes, video. New York: Cornell University, Audio-visual Resource Centre, 1983.

This video looks at the development of the batik industry in Indonesia with a focus on gender issues. *(See 298, 341).*

630. Small Happiness: Women of a Chinese Village. 58 minutes, 16mm/video. Toronto: Full Frame Film and Video Distribution, 1985.

Women of the Long Bow village in China speak about topics that include love and marriage, child bearing and birth control, and work and family relationships. *(See 243, 252, 294).*

631. Surname Viet, Given Name Nam. 108 minutes, 16mm. Vancouver: International Development Education Resource Association, 1989.

This film presents a feminist view of Vietnamese culture, reminding the viewer that, whether 'democratic' or 'socialist', the state is still patriarchal. *(See 336).*

632. Thai Development. 120 minutes, video. Winnipeg: IDEA Centre, n.d.

This six-part film looks at Thai NGO's, rural development, slum development, health and human rights in Thailand. *(See 267, 274, 316, 633).*

633.   Thailand for Sale. 30 minutes, video. Toronto: T.H.A.
        Media Distributors. 1991.

This film provides a critical view of tourism and its impact
on Thailand, in general, and the lives of women, in particular.
(See 267, 274, 316, 632).

634.   Three Generations of Javanese Women. 29 minutes, video.
        New York: Stuart (Martha) Communications Inc., 1980.

In this video, Javanese women discuss how the use of
contraception has changed their lives. *(See 298, 317, 341, 554).*

635.   Who Will Cast The First Stone?. 52 minutes, video.
        Vancouver: International Development Resource Education
        Association, 1988.

This video provides a vivid picture of the Pakistani
women's struggle for equal rights. *(See 260, 276, 618).*

636.   Women in China. 27 minutes, 16mm. Newton:
        Educational Development Centre Inc., 1978.

This production introduces several aspects of change that
have occurred in women's status since the revolution in the
People's Republic of China. *(See 243, 252, 355, 615).*

637.   Women's Rights: India. 30 minutes, video. Toronto: Full
        Frame film and Video Distribution, 1988.

This film focuses on the situation of women in India and
looks at the average women's double work-day. *(See 240, 244,
288, 582, 626).*

6.4 Latin America and the Caribbean

638.   A Time of Daring (Tiempo de Audacia). 40 minutes,
        16mm. Vancouver: International Development Education

Resource Association, 1983.

Provides an intimate portrait of the Salvadorean people and looks at both sides of the War which engulfed their country. *(See 378, 387, 649, 658)*.

639.   Alpaca Breeders of Chimboya.   30 minutes, 16mm. Vancouver: International Development Education Resource Association, 1983.

This film presents the life of a small peasant community in the Andes mountains that depends on the alpaca fleece for its survi val. *(See 380, 406)*.

640.   Broken Silence. 58 minutes, video. Toronto: Full Frame Film and Video Distribution, 1990.

Women come together and, through their quilt work, show what has happened under Pinochet's government in Chile. *(See 370, 379, 626, 642)*.

641.   Castro's Challenge. 60 minutes, video. Winnipeg: IDEA Centre, 1985.

This film explores life in Cuba from the 1950's to the middle of the 1980's. *(See 371, 432, 663)*.

642.   Chile: Four Women's Stories.   25 minutes, video. Cambridge: American Friends Service Committee, 1981 .

Four women speak about their lives before and after September 11, 1973 in Chile. *(See 379, 640)*.

643.   The Companeras Speak. 24 minutes, video. Guatemala News and Information Bureau, 1983.

This video presents Guatemalan women's involvement in the liberation struggle. *(See 424, 429, 651, 670, 672, 675)*.

644.   Debt Crisis: An Unnatural Disaster. 58 minutes, video.
       Toronto: Full Frame Film and Video Production, 1991.

       Focuses on Jamaica and shows that the Caribbean is facing
a turbulent debt crisis which is having a major impact on people's
lives. (See 25, 26, 369, 377, 569, 654, 666, 674).

645.   Dominga. 26 minutes, 16mm/video. Montreal: National
       Film Board of Canada, 1979.

       Focuses on Dominga, the president of a local group, who
helps her people adjust to new methods of food production. (See
436, 440, 662).

646.   The Double Day. 53 minutes, video. New York: Cinema
       Guild, 1975.

       A documentary film which focuses on women's working
conditions in Latin America. (See 370, 375, 403, 445).

647.   Dream of a Free Country: A Message From Nicaragua
       Women. 59 minutes, 16mm/video. Montreal: National
       Film Board of Canada, 1983.

       This film examines the Nicaraguan Revolution from the
eyes of women. (See 368, 530, 653, 676, 677).

648.   Elvia: The Fight For Land and Liberty. 30 minutes, video.
       Vancouver: International Development Education Resource
       Association, 1988.

       Elvia unravels the complex set of factors that contribute to
hunger in the agriculturally abundant land of Honduras. (See 16,
596, 667).

649.   For a Woman in El Salvador Speaking. 7 minutes, video.
       New York: Women Make Movies Inc., 1985.

       This video discusses women's collaboration in fighting

against the abuse of women and children in El Salvador. *(See 378, 387, 638, 658)*.

650. Frida. 108 minutes, 16mm. Vancouver: International Development Education Resource Association, 1987.

The subject of this film is Frida Kahlo, the Mexican painter widely considered to be the most important woman artist of the 20th century. *(See 71, 147)*.

651. Guatemala: Roads of Silence (Caminos del Silencio). 59 minutes, video. Vancouver: International Development Education Resource Association, 1988.

This documentary shows the new forms of social organization that have been developed by the Indians in their daily struggle for survival against a repressive military regime in Guatemala. *(See 424, 429, 643, 670, 672, 675)*.

652. Hell to Pay: Bolivia and the International Monetary Fund. 57 minutes, video. Toronto: Full Frame Film and Video Distribution, 1988.

The working women of Bolivia tell the viewers how the fluctuations in the world economy affect their daily lives. *(See 84, 137, 140, 374, 377, 402)*.

653. Home Life. 27 Minutes, video. Toronto: Full Frame Film and Video Distribution, 1985.

This video depicts the experiences of a peasant family in Nicaragua. *(See 84, 368, 580, 657, 654)*.

654. Living at Risk: The Story of a Nicaraguan Family. 60 minutes, 16mm. Vancouver: International Development Education Resource Association, 1985.

This film provides a sense of the fabric of the everyday life in Nicaragua. *(See 368, 580, 647, 653)*.

655. Love, Women and Flowers. 58 minutes, video. Toronto:
      Full Frame Film and Video Distribution, 1990.

This video focuses on Colombia and provides a detailed
picture of the production of the carnation flower which is marketed
worldwide. *(See 7, 12, 403, 445, 646)*.

656. Las Madres: The Mothers of Piaza de Mayo. 64 minutes,
      16mm. Vancouver: International Development Education
      Resource Association, 1985.

This documentary is about the protest of the mothers of the
30,000 people who disappeared in Argentina during the wave of
kidnapping and murder carried out in the 1970's by the
Argentinean military government. *(See 378, 387, 665, 680)*.

657. Manduti: A Paraguayan Lace.   17 minutes, 16mm.
      Teaneck: C/K productions, 1978.

This audio-visual looks at lace-making and the daily life of
rural women in Paraguay. *(See 271)*.

658. Maria's Story.   53 minutes, 16mm.   Vancouver:
      International Development Education Resource Association,
      1990.

This documentary of a 39 year-old woman, Maria Serrano,
reveals a great deal of information about the poverty and war that
has shaped her life in El Salvador. *(See 84, 137, 378, 387, 633,
649)*.

659. Miss Amy and Miss May. 40 minutes, video. Toronto:
      Full Frame Film and Video Distribution, 1990.

This documentary presents Jamaica's history as told through
the eyes of two remarkable women who played a major role in
shaping their country. *(See 84, 137, 369, 644)*.

660. Monitos: Portrait of an Artisan Family.   11 minutes,

16mm. Studio City: Filmfair Communications, 1974.

This audio-visual shows the home process of forming, firing, painting and marketing of the clay in Mexico. *(See 666).*

661. La Operacion. 40 minutes, video. New York: Cinema Guild, 1982.

This video explores the controversial use of sterilization as a means of population control in Puerto Rico. *(See 13, 346, 665, 671).*

662. Popular Education in Central America. 16 minutes, Slide Tapes. Vancouver: International Development Education Resource Association, 1983.

This slide tape show provides a unique look at the role of the 'popular' methods of education in Central America. *(See 438, 645).*

663. Portrait of Teresa. 103 minutes, 16mm. Toronto: Full Frame Film and Video Distribution, 1979.

This film looks at the multiple roles of Cuban women and shows that patriarchal domination remains even in Socialist Cuba. *(See 371, 432, 641).*

664. The Real Thing. 36 minutes, 16mm. Vancouver: International Development Education Resource Association, 1984.

This film documents a struggle between a large corporation and several hundred Guatemalan workers who are fighting for their jobs, their union and their lives. *(See 424, 429, 643, 651).*

665. Roses in December. 56 minutes, video. New York: First Run Films, 1982.

This video provides a thought provoking comment on U.S.

policy in Puerto Rico, Central America. *(See 368, 387,661, 671)*.

666.   Sabina Sanchez--The Art of Embroidery. 22 minutes, 16mm. Santa Monico: The Works, 1976.

This audio-visual shows the life and work of a woman who makes the embroidered blouses in her village in Mexico. *(See 403, 445, 660, 679)*.

667.   Seeds of Revolution. 28 minutes, 16mm. Vancouver: International Development Education Resource Association, 1979.

The various aspects of Honduras society are examined through interviews with people from all walks of life. *(See 34, 137, 648)*.

668.   Sweet Sugar Rage. 42 minutes, video. Toronto: Full Frame Film and Video Distribution, 1986.

This video presents the harsh conditions facing the female workers on a Jamaican sugar plantation. *(See 16, 369, 644, 674)*.

669.   Tanowitz, Wendy (ed.). Access to Films on Central America. CISPES/ Northwest Regional Office, Oakland, CA., 1984.

670.   Todos Santos Cuchumatan: Report from a Guatemalan Village. 41 minutes, 16mm. Vancouver: International Development Education Resource Association, 1982.

This film presents the life of a village in Guatemala and shows how it is undergoing rapid changes. *(See 424, 429, 643, 651, 672)*.

671.   The Two Worlds of Angelita. 73 minutes, 16mm. New York: First Run Films, 1982.

The story of a young Puerto Rican family who live in two

cultures- their own and the American one is presented in this audio-visual. *(See 368, 387, 661, 665, 675)*.

672. Under the Gun: Democracy in Guatemala. 40 minutes, 16mm/video. Toronto: Full Frame Film and Video Distribution, 1988.

A comprehensive picture of the military rule in Guatemala is presented in this film. *(See 624, 629, 643, 651, 672, 670, 675)*.

673. Union Rights: Bolivia. 30 minutes, video. Toronto: Full Frame Film and Video Distribution, 1988.

This video conveys the violation of the workers' rights in Bolivia by showing their poor working conditions. *(See 380, 439)*.

674. We Run Things. 30 minutes, video. Winnipeg: IDEA Centre, 1991.

Jamaican women who work in the Free Trade zones organize their own collective and establish cooperative housing projects. *(See 644, 668)*

675. When the Mountains Tremble. 85 minutes, 16mm. Vancouver: International Development Education Resource Association, 1983.

This film focuses on the life story of one Indian peasant woman and reveals the rich and complex nature of Guatemalan society. *(See 424, 429, 643, 651, 671, 672)*.

676. Women in Arms. 60 minutes, 16mm. Garrison: Hudson River Film and Video, 1980.

In this film the focus is on the role of women in the 1978-79 Nicaraguan Revolution. *(See 368, 580, 647, 653, 677)*.

677. Women in Nicaragua. 18 minutes, slide tapes. Vancouver: International Development Education Resource Association,

1983.

This slide tape show explores the involvement of Women in Nicaragua, before, during and after the 1979 Revolution. *(See 368, 580, 647, 653, 696).*

678.   Women of the Planet (Mujeres del Planeta). 28 minutes, video. New York: Women Make Movies, 1984.

This video shows women's attempt to organize in a shantytown outside Lima, Peru. *(See 384, 385, 401, 574).*

679.   Working Women: Pottery Making in Amatenango Del Valle. 20 minutes, video. New York: Bruno, Mike, 1980.

A detailed examination of Mayan pottery making is offered in this video. *(See 660, 666).*

680.   The Yankee Years. 60 minutes, video. Winnipeg: IDEA Centre, 1985.

This film chronicle 60 years of U.S. involvement in Central America. *(See 387).*

6.5 The Middle East

681.   A Veiled Revolution. 26 minutes, video. New York: Icarus Films, 1982.

This film looks at Egyptian women who have decided to adopt Islamic dress. *(See 458, 464, 481, 485, 499, 544, 686, 690).*

682.   Biba. 60 minutes, 16mm. Brooklyn: Alden Films, 1980.

This audio-visual shows how war affects people by focusing on an Israeli woman and her family in a small farming village in Israel. *(See 514, 551).*

683.   Children of Fire.   52 minutes, video.   Vancouver:
       International Development Education Resource Association,
       1991.

       This documentary presents a vivid insider's view of the
Intifada.   *(See 459)*.

684.   Factories for the Third World: Tunisia.   43 minutes, video.
       New York: Icarus Films, 1979.

       This video presents a picture of Tunisian women's role in
the international division of labour.   *(See 12, 410, 566)*.

685.   Gaza Ghetto.   82 minutes,16mm/video.   Vancouver:
       International Development Education Resource Association,
       1989.

       Some of the women involved in grassroots organization are
looked at in this film.   *(See 463, 484)*.

686.   The Price of Change.   26 minutes, 16mm.   Vancouver:
       International Development Education Resource Association,
       1982.

       This film focuses on Egypt and presents a picture of the
changing attitudes toward work, the family, sex, and women's
place in Egyptian society.   *(See 451, 458, 503, 513, 516, 521,
681, 690)*.

687.   Ramparts of Clay.   85 minutes, 16mm.   New York: Almi
       Libra Cinema 5 Films (no date).

       This film focuses on Tunisia and Algeria and presents the
story of a young woman who questions her traditional role.   *(See
492, 497, 515, 547)*.

688.   Story of Islam.   120 minutes, video.   Toronto: T.H.A.
       Media Distributors, 1990.

This video presents the history, culture and philosophies of the Islamic faith. *(See 468, 469, 471, 495, 506)*.

689.   Talking to the Enemy: Voices of Sorrow and Rage. 54 minutes, video. New York: Filmakers Library, 1988.

In this production, a young Palestinian journalist and an older Israeli editor try to negotiate their own peace. *(See 463, 484)*.

690.   Village Women in Egypt. 29 minutes, 16 mm. New York: Stuart (Martha). Communications Inc., 1975.

A group of women in Egypt, from various walks of life, talk about their lives and concerns. *(See 458, 681, 686)*.

691.   Women of Lebanon. 58 minutes, video. Toronto: T.H.A. Media Distributors, 1991.

A remarkable picture of women in Lebanon who have emerged to lead their society is provided in this video. *(See 463, 484)*.

692.   Women Under Siege. 26 minutes, 16mm. Vancouver: International Development Education Resource Association, 1982.

This film shows the central role of women in the Palestinian community in Lebanon. *(See 463, 484, 525, 549)*.

693.   Young Women and Tradition: Javonmard (O Zanon-e-Javon). 20 minutes, 16mm. Pittsburgh: Klionsky, Ruth., 1977.

This documentary is about the changing role of women in the Zagros mountain of Iran. *(See 472, 531, 533)*.

Appendix: Women's Organisations and Research Centres

General

Alliance Internationale des Femmes (IAF), P.O. Box 355, Valetta, Malta.

American Friends Service Committee, Nationwide Women's Program, 1501 Cherry St., Philadelphia, PA 19102.

Associazione Italiana Donne per lo Sviluppo, Piazza Capranica 95, interno 4, 00186 Rome, Italy.

Centre for Development and Research, 9 Ny Kongensgade, 1472 Copenhagen K, Denmark.

Centro de Estudios 'Elsa Bergamaschi,' Via della Colonna Antonina 41, Rome, Italy.

Church Women United. 475 Riverside Drive, New York, N.Y. 10115.

Coalition for Women in International Development, c/o OEF International, 2101 L St., NW, Suit 916, Washington, D.C. 20037.

Collectif des Femmes Maghrebines, c/o Maison des Femmes, 8 Cite Prost, 75011 Paris, France.

Federation Democratique Internationale des Femmes, 13 Unter den

Linden, D-1080 Berlin, East Germany.

Fenton, Thomas P. and Mary J. Heffron. Third World Resource Directory: A Guide to Organization and Publications. New York: Orbis Books, 1984.

Giles, Shirley. The Third World Directory: A Guide to Organizations Working for Third World Development. London: Directory of Social Change Publications, 1990.

Institute for Policy Studies, Third World Women's Project, 1901 Q St., NW, Washington, D.C. 20009.

Institute of Development Studies, Program on Women and Development, University of Sussex, Brighton BN1 9RE, England.

Institute of Social Studies, Women's Studies Programme, Badhuisweg 251, 2597 JR the Hague, Netherlands.

International Centre for Research on Women, 1010 16 St., NW, Washington, D.C. 20036.

International Council of Women (ICW), 13 rue Caumartin, 75009 Paris, France.

International Women's Tribute Centre, 777 United Nations Plaza, New York, NY 10017.

International Women's Watch, 464 19 St., Oakland, CA 94612.

International Working Group on Women and the Family, 245A Coldharbour Lane, London SW9 8RR England.

Isis: International, Via Santa Maria dell'Anima 30, 00186 Rome, Italy.

Isis-WICCE: Women's International Cross-Cultural Exchange, Case Postale 2471, CH-1211 Geneva 2, Switzerland.

MADRE, c/o Women's Peace Network, 853 Broadway, New York, NY 10003.

Match International Centre, 171 Nepean St., No. 401, Ottawa, Ontario, K2P 0B4 Canada.

National Institute for Women of Color, 1712 N St., NW, Washington, DC 20036.

Office of Women in International Development, University of Illinois at Urbana-Champaign, 801 S. Wright St., 324 Coble Hall, Champaign, IL 61820.

Presbyterian Church (USA), Third World Women's Coordinating Committee, 475 Riverside Dr., New York, NY 10115.

Progressive Women's Organization, Faelledvej 16 C, 4 tv., DK-2200 Copenhagen, Denmark.

Third World Resources: A Quarterly Review of Resources from and About the Third World. Four issues/year. Newsletter.

Third World Women's Archives, P.O. Box 159, Bush Terminal Sta., Brooklyn, NY 11232.

UNESCO Population Division, 7, Place de Fontenoy, 75700 Paris, France.

United Nations Industrial Development Organization, Program for Women, Vienna International Centre, P.O.Box 300, A-1400 Vienna, Austria.

Wiser Links: Women's International Information Exchange/Resource Centre, 173 Archyway Road, London, N6 England.

Women and Development Network of Australia, 262 Pitt St., Sidney, NSW 2000, Australia.

Women and Development Working Group, Canadian Council for International Cooperation, 450 Rideau St., Ottawa, Ontario K1N 5Z4, Canada.

Women and Work Hazards Group, British Society for Social Responsibility in Science, 9 Poland St., London W1, England.

Women in International Development, Michigan State University, 202 Centre for International Programs, East Lansing, MI 48824-1035.

Women in the World, Curriculum Resource Project, 1030 Spruce St., Berkeley, CA 94707.

Women in World Area Studies, c/o Susan Gross or Marjorie Bingham, 6425 W. 33 St., St.Louis Park, MN 55426.

Women Strike for Peace, National Office, 145 S. 13 St., Philadelphia, PA 19107.

Woman to Woman, 5825 Telegraph Ave., P.O.Box A, Oakland, CA 94609.

Women's Global Network on Reproductive Rights, P.O.Box 4098, Minahassastraat 1, 1009 AB Amsterdam, Netherlands.

Women's International League for Peace and Freedom, 1213 Race St., Philadelphia, PA 19107.

Women's International Network, 187 Grant St., Lexington, MA 02173.

Women's International Resource Exchange, 2700 Broadway, New York, NY 10025.

Women's International Self-Education Resource Links, 173 Archway Rd., London, N16 5AB England.

Women's Research and Resource Centre, 190 Upper St., London

N1, England.

Women's Research Centre in Social Science, H.C. Andersens
Blvd. 38, Nezz., DK-1553, Copenhagen V, Denmark.

Workgroup on Prostitution, Tourism, and Traffic in Women, c/o
MIAC, Voor Clarenburg 10, Utrecht, Netherlands.

World Council of Churches, Women's Desk, 1211 Geneva 20,
Switzerland.

Africa

African National Congress, Women's Section, P.O.Box 31791,
Lusaka, Zambia.

African Training and Research Centre for Women, P.O.Box 3001,
Addis Ababa, Ethiopia.

Association of African Women for Research and Development
(AAWord), B.P. 11007, CD Annexe, Dakar, Senegal.

Center for Women's Studies, University of South Africa, P.O.Box
392, Pretoria 0001, South Africa.

Council for the Development of Economic and Social Research in
Africa (CODESRIA), B.P. 3304, Dakar, Senegal.

Federation of African Media Women, c/o Zimbabwe Inter-Africa
News Agency, P.O.Box 8166, Causeway, Harare, Zimbabwe.

International Defense and Aid Fund for Southern Africa, Women's
Committee, P.O.Box 17, Cambridge, MA 02238.

Maendeleo Ya Wanawake Organisation, P.O.Box 44412, Nairobi,
Kenya.

Mazingira Institute, P.O.Box 14550, Nairobi, Kenya.

South African Council of Churches, Home and Family Life, Women's Desk, P.O.Box 4921, Johannesburg 2000, South Africa.

Women in Development Program, Eastern and Southern African Management Institute (ESAMI), P.O.Box 3030, Arusha, Tanzania.

Women in Development Research Unit, Center for Inter-Racial Studies, Box M.P.167, Mount Pleasant, Salisbury, Zimbabwe

Women in Nigeria, P.O.Box 253, Samaru, Zaria, Kaduna State, Nigeria.

Women's Research and Documentation Center, Institute of African Studies, University of Ibadan, Ibadan, Nigeria.

Women's Research and Documentation Project, Box 35185, University of Dar es Salaam, Dar es Salaam, Tanzania.

Zimbabwe Women's Bureau, 152b Victoria St., Salisbury, Zimbabwe.

Asia

Anveshi Research Centre for Women's Studies, Osmania University Campus, Hyderabad-500007, India.

Applied Socio-Economic Research, Flat No.8, 2nd Floor Sheraz Plaza, P.O.Box 3154, Gulberg, Lahore, Pakistan.

Asian and Pacific Centre for Women and Development, Asian and Pacific Development Centre, Pesiaran Duta, P.O.Box 2224, Kuala, Lumpur, Malaysia.

Asian-Pacific Women's Network, c/o ACFOD, P.O. Box 2930 Bangkok 10500, Thailand.

Asian Women's Institute, c/o Lucknow Publishing House, 37 Cantonment Rd., Lucknow, India.

Asian Women's Research and Action Network, c/o Philipina, P.O. Box 208, Davao City 9501, Philippines.

Centre for Women's Development Studies, B-43, Panchsheel Enclave, New Delhi 110017, India.

Center for Women's Research, Sri Lanka Association for the Advancement of Science, 120/10 Wijerama Mawatha, colombo 7, Sri Lanka.

Centre for Women's Resources, 43 Roces Ave., Mar Santos Bldg., Quezon City, Philippines.

Centre for Women's Studies and Development, Banaras Hindu University, 228 Faculty of Social Sciences, Varanasi 221005, India.

Committe for Asian Women (CAW), 57 Peking Rd., 5/F. Kowloon, Hong Kong.

Committe on Women in Asian Studies (CWAS), 409 Maxwell Hall, Syracuse University, Syracuse, NY 13210.

Concerned Asian Women, Pernambucodreef 27, 3563 CS Utrecht, Netherlands.

Development Institute for Women in Asia (DWIA), The Philippines Women's University, Taft Ave., Manila, Philippines.

Fenton, Thomas P. and Mary J. Heffron. 1986. Asia and Pacific: A Directory of Resources. London: Zed Books.

GABRIELA (General Assembly Binding Women for Reforms, Integrity, Equality, Leadership and Action), Rm, 221, PC1 Bldg., Greenhills Commercial Centre, San Juan, Metro Manila, Philippines.

Gender Roles Research Programme, Centre for Hong Kong Studies, The Chinese University of Hong Kong, Shatin, New

Territories, Hong Kong.

Indian Council of Social Science Research, Women's Studies Programme, IIPA Hostel, Indraparastha Estate, Ring Rd., New Delhi 110002, India.

Indian Social Institute, Programme for Women's Development, Lodi Rd., New Delhi 110003, India.

Institute for Social Research and Education, Carol Mansion, 35 Sitladevi Temple Rd., Mahim, Bombay 400016 India.

Institute of Social Studies Trust, Women's Studies Programme, 5 Deen Dayal Upadhyay Marg, SMM Theatre Crafts Bldg., New Delhi 110002, India.

Institute of Women's Studies. St. Scholastica's College, P.O.Box 3153, Manila, Philippines.

International Women's Studies Institute. 71 Satmasjid Road, Dhanmandi R.A. Dhaka, Bangladesh.

Kali for Women, N84 Panchshila Park, New Delhi 110017, India.

Kanita Project, Universiti Sains Malaysia, School of Social Sciences, Penang, Malaysia.

Korean Women's Institute, EWHA Women's University, Seoul, Korea.

Manushi, C1/ 202 Lajpat Nagar, New Delhi 110024, India.

Martec Center for the Advancement of Women, 25 Cathedral Road, Madras, India.

Pacific and Asian Women's Forum, 4 Bhagwandas Rd., New Delhi 110001, India.

Pacific and Asian Women's Forum (PAWF) 623/27 Rajagiriya

Gardens, Rajagiriya, Sri Lanka.

Pakistan Women's Institute, 93 Jail Rd., Lahore, Pakistan.

Research Center for Asian Women, Sookmyung Women's University, No.53-12,2-Ka Chungpa-Dong, Yongsan-Ku, Seoul, Korea.

Research Center for Women's Studies, SNDT Women's University, Sir Vithadas Vidyavidhar, Santa Cruz West, Juhu Road, Bombay 400049, India.

Research Center on Women, 6 Qinh Cong Trang, Hanoi, Vietnam.

Research Program on Gender and Society, National Tsing Hua University, 101, Sec.2, Kuang Fu Rd., Hsinchu, Taiwan 30043.

Third World Movement Against the Exploitation of Women (TW-MAE-W), P.O.Box 1434, Manila 2800, Philippines.

Voice of Women, 16/1, Don Carolis Rd., Colombo, 5 Sri Lanka.

Women and Development Unit (WAND), University of the West Indies, Extra-Mural Department, Pinelands, St. Michael, Barbados.

Women for Development, Road no. 4, House no. 67, Dhanmondi R.A., Dhaka, Bangladesh.

Women for Women: A Research and Study Group. 15 Green Square, Green Road, Dhaka, Bangladesh.

Women in Development Consortium, Thammasat University, Bangkok, Thailand.

Women in Development Program, Asian and Pacific Development Center, Pesiaran Duta, P.O.Box 12224, 50770, Kuala Lumpur, Malaysia.

Women's Action for Development, D-139 Anand Niketan, New

Delhi 110021, India.

Women's Centre, 307 Yasmeen Apartment, Yeshwant Nagar, Vakola, Santacruz (W), Bombay 400055, India.

The Women's Committee of the United Nations, Association of the Republic of China, 101 Ning Po West Street, Taipei, Taiwan.

Women's Information Centre, 2/3 Soi Wan Lang, Arunamarin Rd., Bangkok 10700, Thailand.

Women's Link, Women's Concern Desk, Christian Conference of Asia, 480, Lorong 2, Toa Payoh, Singapore 1231, Singapore.

Women's Research and Development Center, Prince of Songkla University, Faculty of Management Science, Head Yai 90112, Thailand.

Women's Resource and Research Center, Katipunan Parkway, Loyola Heights, Quezon City, Philippines.

Women's Studies Program, Faculty of Social Sciences, Chiangmai university, Thailand.

Women's Studies Unit, Tata Institute of Social Sciences, P.O. Box 8313 Sion-Trombay Road, Deonar, Bombay 400088, India.

Latin America and the Caribbean

AMES: Salvadoran Women's Association. P.O.Box 40311, San Francisco, CA 94140

ASESORA: Centro Nacional para el Desarrollo de la Mujer y la Famila. (National Center for the Development of Women and the Family), Ministeriio de Cultura, Juventud y Deporte, apartado 10.227-1000, San Jose, Costa Rica.

Association of University Women in Honduras, El Centro,

Tegucigalpa, D.C. Casa No. 1241 y 7a Ave., Honduras.

Caribbean Association for Feminist Research and Action (CAFRA), Language Laboratory, University of West Indies, St. Augustine, Trinidad and Tobago.

Carlos Chaga Foundation. Avenue Professor Francisco Morato 1565, Sao Paulo 05513, Brazil.

Centre de Estudia y Atencion del Nino y la Mujer (Centre for the Study of Women and Children), Enrique Foster Sur 24, Dpto. 10, Santiago, Chile.

Centre de Estudios de la Mujer (Center for Women's Studies), Bellavista 0547, Santiago, Chile.

Center for Economic Development Studies (CEDE), University of Los Andes, Apartado Aereo 4976, Bogota, Columbia.

Centro Ecuatariano pa la Promocion accion de la Mujer, Los Rios (Ecuadorian Center for the Promotion and Action of Women) 2238 y Gandara, Apartado Postal 182-C, Secursal 15, Quito, Ecuador.

Centro de Estudios de la Mujer, Olleros 2554-P.B., 1426 Buenos Aires, Argentina.

Centro de Informacion y Desarrolle de la Mujer (CIDEM). Casilla de Correo 3961, La Paz, Bolivia.

Centro de Informacion y Recursos para La Mujer, Calle 36, No. 17-44, Bogota, Colombia.

Centro de Investigacion para la Accion Femenina (CIPAF), Apartado Postal 1744, Santo Domingo DN, Dominican Republic.

Centro de la Mujer Peruana 'Flora Tristan,' Jiron Quilca 431, 100 Lima, Peru.

Centro de Promocion de la Mujer. Casilla 21170, La Paz, Bolivia.

Centro Paraguay de Estudios de la Mujer (Paraguayan Center for Women's Studies) Facultadad de Derecho, Universidad Catolica, CC 1718 Asuncion, Paraguay.

Circulos Femeninos Populares, Apartado 4240, 1010-A Caracas, Venezuela.

Comunicacion, Intercambio y Desarrollo Humano en America Latina (CIDHAL). Apartado Postal 579, Cuernavaca, Morelos, Mexico.

DAWN (The Development alternative with Women for a New Era). c/o Women and Development Unit, School of Continuing Studies, university of the West Indies, Pinelands, St. Michael, Barbados.

Equipo de Investigacion Asistencia para la Mujer (Research Team for women's Association). Beruti 3032, c.p. Buenos Aires 1425.

Fenton, Thomas P. and Mary J. Heffron. 1986. Latin America and Caribbean: A Directory of Resources. London: Zed Books.

Flora Tristan Peruvian Women's Center, Parque Hernan Velarde 42, Lima 1, Peru.

Fundacao Carlos Chagas Women's Program, Avenida Prof. Francisco Morato 1565, 05513 Sao Paulo SP, Brazil.

Grupo Estudio la Condicion de la Mujer en Uruguay (GRECMU), (Group for the Study of Women in Uruguay), Juan Pamillier 1174, Montevideo, Uruguay.

Grupo de Estudio de la Mujer Paraguaya (Group for the Study of Women in Paraguay), Eligio Ayala 973 C.C. 2157, Asuncion, Paraguay.

Interdisciplinary Program on Women's Studies, El Colegio de Mexico, Camino al Ajusco No. 20, C.P. 01000, Mexico D.F., Mexico.

International Research and Training Institute for the Advancement of Women (INSTRAW), Avenida Cesar Nicolas Penson 102-A, P.O. Box 21747, Santo Domingo, Dominican Republic.

Isis Internacional, Casilla 2067, Correo Central, Santiago, Chile.

Nucleos de Estudios Sobre a Mulher (Centre for the Study of Women), The Potifical Catholic University, Rua Marques de Sao Vicente, 225 Gavea, Rio de Janiero 22453, Brazil.

Programa de Informacion para la Mujer (Women's Information Program, National University), Apartado 1009, Centro Colon, San Jose, Costa Rica.

Programa Interdisciplinario de Estudios de Genero. (Interdisciplinary Program for the Study of Gender), Universidad de Costa Rica, San Jose, Costa Rica.

Unidad de Comunicadion Alternativa de la Mujer. Casilla 16-637, Correo 9, Santiago, Chile.

Women for Guatemala, P.O.Box 53421, 1618 V St., NW, Washington, D.C. 20009.

The Middle East

Ahfad University for Women, P.O.Box 167, Omdurman, Sudan.

All of Tunia Women for Research and Information on Women, 7 Rue Sinan Pacha, Tunis.

Arab Women Solidarity Association (AWSA). 25 Murad Street, Giza, Egypt.

Center for Egyptian Civilization Studies, 18, Saray el Guezireh, Apt. 7, Cairo Zamalek, Egypt.

Center for Women's Studies, P.O.Box 13145-654, Tehran, Iran.

General Arab Women Federation, Hay A-Maghreb, Mahaela 304, Zuqaq 5/33, Baghdad, Iraq.

Institute for Women's Studies in the Arab World, Beirut University College, P.O. Box 13-5053, Beirut, Lebanon.

International Network for Sex Equity in Education, 22 Yahuda Halevi St., Raanana 43556, Israel.

Najda: Women Concerned about the Middle East, P.O.Box 7152, Berkeley, CA 94707.

Sudan Women's Research and Development Organization, P.O.Box 2081, Khartoum, Sudan._

Women Against the Occupation, P.O. Box 2760, Tel Aviv, Israel.

Women Living Under Muslim Laws, 34980 Combailleaux (Montpellier).

Women's Studies Program, University of Haifa, Mt. Carmel, Haifa 31999, Israel.

Author Index

Country and Region Index

Subject Index

About the Compiler

PARVIN GHORAYSHI is Associate Professor of Sociology at the University of Winnipeg. Her teaching and research are in the areas of the sociology of work, social theory, and economic sociology. She is currently working on a research project on women and work in the Middle East.